Vagabonds
in
France

Michael A. Barry

This book is dedicated to all those who live to travel
and love to experience and understand different cultures.
To the wanderlust in all of us.
Bon Voyage, Happy Trails, Fair Winds!

Contents

Acknowledgments

I like to thank all those who were part of this process:

My beta readers:

Scott King

Nancy Mackay

Scott and Donna

Lisa Angermann

Elke Sundermann, editor

Liesl Walsh, photographer

JC and Isabelle

Marie

Snowflake

Preface

There's always that person, you know the one I'm talking about. When they come back from an exotic vacation, start declaring how wonderful, amazing, and perfect the place was they just got back from? Social media is full of these examples. Well, I have traveled enough to know each destination has its beauty and awesomeness. It also has its, let's say, "deal breakers" for utopia.

This book is a lighthearted attempt to convey a balanced look at the people and places we experienced on this most memorable and unexpected trip to France. Don't get any wrong ideas, I loved France and dream of returning, but cultural differences and the many "what the hell" moments are always good for a few giggles. I hope you enjoy.

Come with us as we lost our home, put everything in storage, and became vagabonds in France. Experience a transatlantic ocean-crossing, navigate through Europe, dodge pickpockets, climb mountains and descend into the Paris Metro.

Endure nasty weather and illness, witness the flood of the century, and meet some wonderful and not-so-wonderful people. Live among the French and try to learn their ways and language. Then make it back home to an empty house we'd never seen before.

Hi, my name is Michael Barry, I'm 53 and live in Florida with my wife of 21 years, Lisa. We are semi-retired, or otherwise known as "in-between careers" and just trying to figure some things out. We sold our home and business in Pennsylvania in 2009 and moved to Florida. I just couldn't take the northeast winters anymore, so we sold half of our stuff, packed up the rest, and headed to the land of endless summers, ocean breezes, and sandy beaches with Jimmy Buffet music playing in the background. Well, that was our plan.

We spent the first three years living on the east coast of Florida, in two different houses. After we fixed up our dream house, it regrettably ended up being a "flipper". That story could be the subject for another book. We decided the east coast of Florida just wasn't our cup of tea anyway, so we packed up again and headed to Parrish, Florida, just south of Tampa.

I had some health problems for a few years, but a month before we got "the call", my health took a wonderful turn for the better. I started to get a new lease on life, a renewed hope. I always loved to travel since I was a young man, and while I was sick I had serious regrets about not doing what I love the most in life, and that was to see the world. With this gift of a second chance, combined with the "lemon" we received in the form of a phone call, find out how we made lemonade, ala Français.

This book started out a modest journal designed only to help us catalog pictures during the trip. When family and friends discovered our plans, they insisted we send plenty of pictures. Since I was cataloging tons of pictures and on the computer anyway for the updates, I might as well tell a few of the interesting stories during the trip. Do you see where this is going?

When we got home, those on the receiving end of our updates told us how much they loved them, and how they experienced the trip with us. With encouraging words from friends and family, plus already having a foundation of a sixty-seven page "journal", what the heck, I might as well turn it into a book. Besides, it was fun doing the updates.

Before we left, I heard a lot about the bathroom situation in Europe, both in sheer lack and gender mixing. We first encountered our first real "what the hell" moment with bathrooms at the Avignon Bridge in Provence. We decided to include this account and others in a Bathroom Report section for our emails home, and it was a big hit. We learned quickly in France, if you see a public toilette you better use it. You may not see another one the rest of the day when you desperately need it!

When Lis and I travel, we try to go native as much as possible. To save money, we'd make our own meals, stay at B&B's or rent monthly apartments, ride public transportation when possible, and basically live as locals and within our means. However, the one thing we couldn't do is to sit for hours at outside cafes just to experience the cafe culture. No no, we had places to go and things to see. Plus I'd rather stick pins in my eyes than to sit that long for the French "meal experience".

Most names in this book have been changed to protect the innocent. (I guess that's what I'm supposed to say anyway.)

I'm of Irish stock, and someone down the line must have kissed the Blarney stone, which means a short story will be a challenge, so please have mercy. The cities you will encounter with us are Key West, Florida, USA; Funchal, Madeira, Portugal; Malaga, Cartagena, and Barcelona, Spain; Antibes, Nice, Èze, St. Paul de Vence, Arles, Avignon, Paris, Giverny, and Versailles, France.

Fasten your seat belts, here we go, enjoy.

Music at the steps of Sacré-Cœur basilica
Montmartre, Paris

Rest not! Life is sweeping by;
Go and dare before you die.
Something mighty and sublime
Leave behind to conquer time.
- Johann Goethe

Chapter 1

Out of Left Field Surprise

November 3rd, 2015: It was a cool Florida winter day, though much warmer than the Philadelphia weather we had escaped from seven years ago, when the phone rang. Lisa answered and mouthed to me it was Vince, our property manager. He never calls us, only emails. As soon as I heard it was Vince and Lisa's tone when she spoke to him, I knew it wasn't good, and we were probably out of here.

Vince told us the owner of our property wanted to sell, but they would of course, honor the remainder of the lease. However, when the house sells, we'd have to go. He also said, if closing was after our lease was up, we could stay as long as we needed to. Thankfully, closing took five months, and we needed every minute of it.

I felt stale where we lived, bored. A change of location would be exciting and invigorating. I looked online at rentals in the surrounding areas to see our options months before he called.

What are we to do? Where do we go? All the rents in Florida jumped about forty to fifty percent this year! Should we move north of Tampa, south of Sarasota or towards the center of the state? Do we consider another state? We've survived so far on the money from the sale of our Pennsylvania house. However, we're not investment bankers with bailout money, you know?

We investigated the west coast of Florida, to pre-approve areas and neighborhoods. We traveled south to Venice, Nokomis, and North Port, but we just weren't feeling the love. We searched online, and rents were way up all over. It looks like we'd end up paying $400 more per month for the same sized or smaller house. Things weren't looking good.

We were frustrated, just imagining living in a smaller place for more money brought us down. One day, I said to Lis, "Let's consider our options. We have to live somewhere, right? Who says we have to live in the U.S.? . . . What about, say . . . I don't know . . . . We could live on the road a while . . . . How about Europe? . . . How about France?" Lis looked up to the ceiling, calculated some things in her head, and said, "I don't know, let me think about it?"

We have to pack and move anyway, why not put all our stuff in storage and just go. I love to travel and toured Europe in the early 90's for fourteen incredible days, and always swore I'd go back.

Since my health has improved, this may be my last chance! Besides, this area is getting a little stale.

Traveling is what I truly love. I've been to the Middle East, Europe, South America, Mexico and about fifteen Caribbean islands, but never made it to Paris or anywhere in France. I've heard so much about it, we just had to do it. Visiting Paris was on my "rich guy's bucket list" and so was an entire summer in Europe, but since I wasn't rich, it was only a pipe dream, or was it?

If we put all of our furniture in storage, we won't have rent to pay in the U.S. If we're not paying rent, we might as well travel and knock a few countries off the ole bucket list. We can travel as long as our bodies will let us. So we won't even consider securing our new place in Florida, until we decide to come back. Furnished vacation rentals are abundant during the low season, we could grab a one or two month lease while we search for something more permanent.

Flights to Europe have been pretty expensive the past decade. You know, I always wanted to do a repositioning cruise across the Atlantic. I priced around, and wouldn't you know? Royal Caribbean would take our two homeless old bodies from nearby Tampa Bay on a repositioning cruise across the Atlantic for two whole weeks. Lis was coming around to the idea.

Royal Caribbean would feed and entertain us, stop at two islands, and three historic mainland cities in Spain. At the end of the cruise, they'd drop us off in Barcelona all for the same price as two one-way tickets to Europe. Since Barcelona is just a hop, skip, and a jump from the border of southern France, this is starting to look like a plan? Lis is all in, we're going!

The planning was almost a full-time job: we had to book the cruise, research B&B's, read reviews, plan days with trains and bus schedules/tickets, secure flights, find plant sitters, exercise for all the walking we'll be doing, and, oh yeah, learn a little French. All this while moving our stuff.

We didn't know anybody well enough to just hand off our beloved banana plants for such a long time. We had no idea when we'd be back, and didn't want to burden anyone with the responsibility of watering these guys every three days for three months. We owned these plants since Pennsylvania. Imagining the tropics through them pulled us through some long, cold, depressing winters.

This is what we did, and don't tell anybody: there's an unfinished development about a mile down the road from us which was overgrown. One Sunday we located an out-of-the-way place, dug a couple of holes and relocated the plants. We're taking risks here (one is trespassing), but it was either plant them or throw them away, so we took the chance.

Lisa LOVES photography. She doesn't use a smartphone for pictures, she uses the "old-fashioned" digital cameras from the good ole days. After a day of shooting, she'd come home and upload her memory card to the computer and jazz 'em all up with special effect software. When you edit fancy pictures the way she does, you have to take them in a format called "raw", which uses about twenty-five megabytes per picture. It adds up fast.

Now if she's going to be using up so much space, we're going to need an external hard drive. Since you just can't go from camera to external, you need a computer in-between. We're going to need a light travel computer, and my laptop weighs about 92 pounds, so that won't work. For travel, we settled on a Macbook, which weighs in the neighborhood of 7 grams, and an external hard drive which weighs 8 grams. Go figure? (*Weights and measure of these products are for comedic relief only and not to be construed as factual.*)

Blah, blah, blah, tons of planning, selling stuff on Craigslist, rent two storage units a mile apart (long story), and moving a little bit every day with the car. One of our units was a 10 x 15 climate-controlled indoor unit and the other was a 10 x 30 outdoor solar oven, which could handle our car, garage stuff, and remaining belongings if we packed like chipmunks. Storing our car inside our unit was actually cheaper than a separate car storage price; one place wanted $300 a month, and the car would be stored outside . . . IN FLORIDA?

First thing I did was drive to the storage units, and put the shelves together to get the units ready for the moving truck days. I'd drive to the units about five days a week, and the other two days we'd pack. Every other week we'd rent a U-haul truck from our local Ace hardware store and load it up immediately that day with the big stuff.

Early the next morning, we would drive to the unit, unload, and return the truck to its nest all within twenty-four hours. If you plan it right, you're only charged for one day plus mileage. Don't take the scenic route like I did one day, they charge by the mile.

It took four 17-foot U-hauls and 100 car trips to fill up both units, but moving's always a ton of laughs. No, really it wasn't. We had no time to worry about the risks, cutting ties, leaving the country with no return date, just see where the wind takes us, and no definite home to come back to.

Mainland Europe will allow you ninety days within its borders, and afterwards you've overstayed your welcome, now get out. The U.K., on the other hand, will allow you an extra thirty days after the mainland's ninety to hang out for some fish and chips with a pint or two.

Our aim was open-ended: let's see where we end up. We had ambitious plans. After the first two and a half weeks of May in southern France, where it should be warm, we would then travel north to Paris and stay a month till mid June, hoping for at least some summer weather. In Philadelphia, May is really nice, and June is summer, so it should be lovely, right?

After Paris, we made reservations to see the wine and chateau country of the Loire Valley, Normandy and it's military history. After those, our tentative plans included Holland, the country of Lisa's heritage. Then on to England for fish and chips, over to Ireland for a pint, and finally, cross the pond, home to Florida.

Remember, we'll have no rent or bills other than storage. All the money we would have spent living in the U.S., we'd now just use to live over there. Monthly rents are comparable, maybe a smidgen more, but it's now or never. We booked all the way to Normandy, and from there we'll see how we feel.

Every day the house is more sparse. We've learned to live without many of the creature comforts, we have to get used to surviving with less. With just a week to go, we're down to a folding table, chairs, blow-up bed, coffee maker, a few plates, and paper cups.

The day before boarding the cruise ship, we drove to Tampa and rented a car at the closest rental agency to the port. We live just south of Tampa, so it wasn't a problem.

The same day we picked up the rental vehicle, we took both cars to the large outdoor rental, backed our car into the unit, stuffed a Brillo pad into the exhaust (hint: mice), detached the battery terminals, spread moth balls underneath the car (hint: critters), locked it up, double-checked the double locks, and off we went, back to our desolate home for our last night.

Because everything is happening so fast, we didn't have time to process the reality of everything. While we sat on the carpet looking around at the poorly lit, empty house, it really hit us. It was a bit surreal, there's no turning back. We're locked in, and this thing is going to happen. Tomorrow we will be homeless!

Chapter 2

No Turning Back

Leaving Tampa on Transatlantic Cruise to Europe

Saturday, April 16, 2016

Hoping all things go as planned, we sat in our empty house we lived in for three years, and waited for the right time to leave for the Tampa cruise terminal. Around 10 am we headed out the door for the last time. We backed out the driveway, and said "good-bye" to our home of three years and to the memories. We are officially vagabonds, travelers without a permanent home. We drove north on 301 through Brandon, west on 60, and straight to the cruise terminal, where I dropped Lisa off with all our earthly possessions (not in storage).

From the terminal, I drove down a few blocks to return the rental car. I asked the car rental agency the day before about a shuttle to the terminal; they said yes they had one, but what they didn't tell me was, it only stopped by on the hour, and I just missed the most recent van. Great, now I would have to wait 55 minutes or walk 25 minutes in the Florida sun. Since I've been feeling healthier by the day, I decided to walk . . . in the heat . . . no water. Boy this ain't starting off good. Take deep breaths! Center! Deep breaths!

The line to check in was short and easy, security was theater at best. We could have snuck in twice as much booze than we did. Instead of carrying our luggage to our room and having it immediately for use, the cruise line made us hand it over to the valet. It took over five hours to make it to our room. I really could have used a change of clothes because of the hot, humid Florida weather, plus my marathon walk from the car rental agency.

The room was nothing fancy but nice: queen-sized bed, drawers, two port holes, TV, phone, and a bathroom/shower which was a little bit bigger than our last cruise fourteen years ago on another major cruise line. The shower on that ship was so small you had to leave the bathroom just to change your mind.

This recently renovated ship is 915 feet long, ten stories out of water, with four restaurants, two large pools, six whirlpools, lounges, rock climbing wall, casino, bars, fitness center, walking track, and more. The main pool has a big screen TV where we watched a couple movies at night. She can accommodate 2416 guests, not including crew.

It usually takes a few days for me to get my bearings on a ship this big, but it's part of the adventure. Plus it's our home now. Sometimes when you're just going about navigating through the ship, you get disoriented and occasionally have to look out a window to figure what direction is the front of the ship, yeah, it's enormous.

It's been a rough few weeks getting the house ready to move, and packing for our European adventure. We are both exhausted, it's been an intense pace every day, all day long for a few weeks. The last week was the roughest for us. We finished all our packing and most of the cleaning.

I can't believe we are actually "homeless". It felt strange not having an address. We'll live on the ship for two weeks while crossing the Atlantic Ocean to Europe. This is the beginning of a new adventure and a new lease on life. Hopefully we left some of the hard times in Florida, and new and good things are in our future. We love Florida, but we had a couple tough years and need a real change.

It was beautiful to see the Tampa skyline from the bay. From the top deck, you could see so much of the city. Our ship was parked next to a 1940's era "Liberty Ship", which is now a museum. While waiting to leave, another cruise ship did a "K" turn leaving the docks. As we pulled away from the dock, Lisa became a little emotional and teared up. All the emotions of being uprooted and uncertainty finally came to the surface. Come on, Lis, pirates don't cry?

Lis and I were thrilled we'd be sailing under the Sunshine Skyway Bridge and talked about it since we made reservations. We calculated there should be no problem with our dinner schedule and witnessing the ship pass under the bridge. However, our cruise ship departed Tampa an hour later than expected, and we were getting a little nervous. As we pulled away from the dock, the ship blew its enormous horn and scared everyone to death. I really wish I had my change of clothes now. Not to be foiled by the delay, we hustled down to the casual dining room, ate fast, and arrived topside just in time to see the bridge from below.

We traveled many times by car over this breath-taking icon of the tri-city area. With its two mast-like vertical supports and multiple cables descending down on an angle, the bridge looks like a sailboat from a distance. The original Skyway Bridge was destroyed in 1980 when it was struck by a loaded freighter in the fog.

When we finally passed under, the top of the ship came within thirteen feet of touching the bridge, whoa! The Skyway Bridge looks a lot thinner from underneath when it's next to our giant ship. We are now entering the Gulf of Mexico, heading south to Key West, the famous Conch Republic.

Key West and Our Last Day in the U.S.
Sunday Morning, April 17, 2016

Our first stop was Key West, we're regulars there (almost unofficial Conches). We reserved bikes online from home to tour our island. The rental company met us right outside the ship. The young man set us up with two bikes, and we're off to cruise down historic Duval Street, all the way to the iconic southernmost point. I could people watch on Duval all day. Painted people, Hemingway look-alikes, bikers, cross-dressers, street performers and tourists from all over the world cruise this street. We circled around and drove past our old secret hotel from two years ago, the Blue Marlin. She's still looking good. It's not the glitzy Wyndham, but it's a great location, clean, quiet, and the ole gal looks to have a fresh coat of paint recently.

From the Marlin, we split up and Lisa made a beeline to the Ernest Hemingway House and proceeded to take hundreds of wide angle pictures. I made my way to the Key West Butterfly Nature and Conservatory on Duval. They have some amazing butterflies and birds; however, my favorite, the multicolored Lady Gouldian finches, were not part of the flock this year.

This is my favorite stop in Key West, it's a big zen-like experience in a small building. You can walk among the wild birds and butterflies. If you're an extra sweet person, butterflies will land on you and go for a ride as you walk around. You have to check yourself on the way out in a full-length mirror, to make sure you don't take any stowaways home.

Lisa loves the Hemingway House, it just begs you to take pictures of it, with its white exterior, yellow green shutters and second floor wrap-around porch.   You can imagine Papa Hemingway sitting upstairs with his pipe, rocking away on his favorite chair, petting one of his six-toed cats.

After this gnarly pirate's dangerous butterfly excursion, I hopped on my bike and met Lisa at the Hemingway House, and we finished the tour together.   Ernest was a legend here and had the coolest house with the only inground pool in Key West.   The Hemingway house is brimming with character and has the most interesting local folklore. This is our third visit to Papa's house and still enjoyed it.

After 6 hours of visiting some of our old haunts, we parked and locked our bikes at the Custom House, returned the keys to the concierge inside the Westin, and walked right to our awaiting ship for the big Atlantic Ocean crossing. This is our last time on land for the next eight days and U.S. soil for the next two to three months.

As we pulled away from the dock, Lis and I went to the back of the ship to watch the land fade into the distance. Few people joined us there, I guess they were hungry for their first dinner?

With the ship sailing away, we could see the revelers at Mallory Square waiting for the ritual sun-setting festivities. We've experienced that local ritual in person more times than I can remember.

The sun-setting festivities include jugglers, comedians, magicians, trained cats, acrobats, sword-swallowers, and musicians. And as the sun sets, sailboats glide across the horizon. At a certain point, with careful timing, someone starts the ten second countdown, and as the sun slips away, the crowd lets out a rousing cheer. It's a must see, must experience in Key West.

2nd Day at Sea
Tuesday, April 19

We've had high seas the first two days - eight to ten-foot waves. The ship's swaying takes time getting used to. It gets a little tricky to walk up and down the steps when the whole boat is moving. Sometimes you're weightless and light on your feet, other times extremely heavy and walk like you're in cement. Our room is quiet, but we do feel the movement a lot since we are in the bow of the ship (that's front for you landlubbers). The first day we passed by part of the Bahamas in the distance; it will be the last land we see for over a week, which was pretty cool.

We dined in the Windjammer for most of our meals; it's casual all the time. The young people employed on these ships are from all over the world. These kids work hard and long hours. The big Turkish guy, Khalid, who runs the dining room, looks like he could be a tough guy character in a James Bond movie. Don't be afraid, Khalid's smile can light up a room. At the end of the cruise, googly-eyed passengers were taking Khalid's picture just in case he makes it to Hollywood.

3rd Day at Sea
Wednesday, April 20

On these cruise ships they constantly encourage you to wash your hands to stave off the dreaded intestinal viruses. We constantly used their waterless washing stations all over the ship. The ship also employed a gregarious young Russian "washy washy" girl at the entrance to the Windjammer restaurant. She was armed with two containers of waterless bacterial hand wash. She would squirt anyone's palm who held out their hands and she'd say, "Washy, washy!"

Despite washing religiously, I came down with stomach issues, and had to rest in the room most of the third day. I had a slight fever off and on, and was often tired. Gatorade, Tums, and bottled water really helped me feel better. By the afternoon I was able to leave the room to get a meal. We're getting to know some of the young servers and enjoyed talking with them in the Windjammer dining room. Our favorites were:

Joy (25), a Chinese young lady who's mature for her age, a sweet soul, and shared with us about what life is like working on the ship. On occasions if her schedule allowed, she would visit the different ports of call. Later in the cruise when Joy knew Lis wasn't feeling well, she would bring her chamomile tea with two packets of honey without even asking. What a sweetheart. Lis and I would always try to sit in Joy's section.

Jarred (23) is a male Chinese server, he's amiable with a big infectious smile who also enjoys talking with us. Jarred is his English name, he says it's a strong name. He likes the fact Lis and I are patient and encouraging with his English. Jarred is married and has a toddler back in China.

We also met an Indian server named Biju, he told us about the different regions in India and the unique foods in each. He explained how his wife wanted him to work the cruise line to learn about food since she is a chef. Yeah, we thought it was strange also. His wife lives with his parents and brother, so he doesn't have to worry about her.

By now, we are east of the Bahamas, two thousand miles away from Funchal, Portugal, and the bottom of the ocean is five thousand meters down. We are in a less traveled area of the ocean now, so we won't see many more ships like we did a few days ago. However, we did have a large tanker ship to the north of us yesterday for what seemed most of the day. We'd love to see a whale or dolphin sometime, I guess we'll keep looking.

Today the seas were much calmer and easier to handle, however the Captain said tomorrow the seas will be 12-13 feet tall, so it will be rockier and rougher, and cloudy. Today was sunny, so we lingered by the pool in the shade for about an hour to get some fresh salt air. While fiddling with our electronics, we learned how to transfer pictures from our phone to the computer, then on to the external hard drive. Yeah, that's one for the old guy!

4th Day at Sea
Thursday, April 21

The old salty retired dogs get up early to reserve their place and set anchor at the indoor pool. If you get there just a little late, you're out of luck and will end up outside. You can set your watch by these retired guys. The indoor pool seems to be a desirable place for these seasoned citizens, due to low noise factor, out of the direct sun, and of course, close to the little pirates room.

The ship moves the clock ahead 1 hour every other day at noon. Lis says it feels good to be able to stay up late and sleep in, but lunch time is now at breakfast.

Internet is $.69 a minute, $30 for a single day, so we won't be using the net a whole lot during this cruise, who needs the internet anyway? All of our hotels and B&B's in Europe have WiFi, so we'll catch up there. I hear some people would go through major withdrawal without the internet.

Lisa is trying to get used to washing laundry by hand in our bathroom sink. We packed light to remain nimble in Europe, but the cruise was two weeks long. Hanging wet laundry to dry in the shower with clothespins was a bit of a chore. Because of limited space she has to do wash almost daily in small amounts, not fun.

The older cruise ships had coin operated laundries available for you to use yourself for $1.50 to wash, $1.50 to dry. The newer ships have laundry service only through the ship's cash registers at $15 a bag.

On the news today we found out the entertainer Prince died at age 57. : (

Thirteen foot waves today, but the ship's stabilizers took the edge off the battering we were taking. The ship placed barf bags at all the elevators and stairwells, fortunately we witnessed no accidents. Around noon we watched an oil tanker getting a little too close to our ship at the bow. The tanker looked like it was right in our path, but sped up and sailed parallel to us for a while. Everyone took pictures of it, even some of the crew seemed perplexed, but assured us everything was OK (Costa Concordia cough, cough).

It was a dreary, overcast day, so we rested in the afternoon and caught a movie in our cabin. The ship has an English movie channel with a good rotation of movies.

When we walked into the dining room for dinner, we couldn't find Joy, so we just picked a table with an ocean view. We must have been spotted by Biju because he made a beeline right for us. He hung around and told us more things about India, and showed us his wedding pictures of his wife with traditional Indian clothes, jewelry, and henna-dyed skin. It's hard to get a hot meal, because Biju hangs around so long.

Instead of a fancy show tonight, we made our way to the Centrum, the daytime jazz lounge, for some quiet easy listening music. Here in the center of the ship is the tall atrium with seating on every level to watch the stage on the first floor. Of course you have the glass elevators, mirrors, and blinking lights. After a couple hours, when the musicians started to repeat themselves, we made it back to the room, relaxed, and did more laundry.

5th Day at Sea
Friday, April 22

Lis and I aren't into crowds. We've met a lot of wonderful temporary friends on the other cruises we've been on, and this should be the same. We're just cautious lately, and pick and choose our times carefully, though I love to talk to people from other countries.

Today we watched two movies in our room: one about Herman Melville, the author of *Moby-Dick*, and *Brave* about a Scottish princess who wants to change her mom, the queen. Two movies is normally what we watch in as many years.

I ran a slight fever off and on, and my tummy doesn't feel right. I hope I feel better soon, I'm barely eating, and all the food looks so good. Our last cruise a decade ago, I remember the two days at sea seemed to last an eternity. We're double that time at sea now, and it's not that bad, but we really do miss solid earth.

We talked with sweet Joy again today, and found out she thinks Tom Cruise is handsome. Joy asked if we watched any of the ship's movies, and I told her we watched *Concussion*, and Will Smith was from our hometown of Philadelphia. Due to a translation problem, Joy thought I said Will Smith stuck his head out of the TV to say hi to us. I don't know how she came up with that, but we all laughed. Joy told us Jarred was teary eyed last night when his wife called, and his little girl called him "Daddy" for the first time. This explains why he walked around all smiles today!

6th Day at Sea
Saturday, April 23

At lunch, Lis and I both tried the British/Australian condiment known as Marmite, it's a yeast based product I've heard horror stories about for years. Seeing we have people on this ship from all over the world explains why they have this nasty condiment. I opened the protective hazmat cover and took a quick whiff, I jolted my head back and closed my eyes. We both spread a minuscule amount on bread and put it up to our mouths like it was poison. Grimacing at first, because the spread tasted like gasoline or something lubricating a car.

Lis tried it, but didn't like it at all, end of story, no more, nada, nine, non, verboten. Being the trooper that I am, I kept at this devil's concoction in small amounts. Persistence paid off, and I eventually saw the charm. It's earthy, like cilantro or kombucha. We are now six days at sea, and we long for land.

7th Day at Sea
Sunday, April 24

Every time we go to the Windjammer, Biju comes over and butters us up while we're trying to eat. It seems forced, fake. He might assume time spent "bonding" obligates us for a bigger tip. Car salesmen use this technique, more time spent with customer equals obligation to purchase. We'll have to see how that works out for him?

We caught the last half of the movie *The Big Short* on the big screen by the main pool. It was a very small crowd, I guess because there were no explosions or brain-eating aliens invading earth. It was about the insanity of the 2008 housing crisis. I loved it, and can't wait to get home and watch it from the start.

Two days left till Funchal and a welcome break to the eight days at sea. The constant sailing hasn't been too bad, besides our temporary home is a cruise ship, it could be worse. The time changes have messed with our normal life's rhythm lately, it's like daylight savings time every day. Lis has a sore throat now, hoping it goes away before we get to Funchal.

I like to get up early before the beehive starts buzzing. I enjoy my quiet time to study French, use the hot tub, and a workout in the gym. I'll come back to the room for a shower and then head to breakfast together with Lis. We've eaten all our meals at the Windjammer lately, it's less pretentious than the formal dining room. You don't have to sit with strangers, wait for servers, plus I didn't bring a tuxedo.

8th Day at Sea

Monday, April 25

Lis has a cough like so many others on the ship. Someone probably picked up a bug from a grandchild or shopping cart before the cruise. One hug and a kiss from grandma, and "shazam", 5% of the entire ship is coughing now. No washy washy girl can stop an airborne virus like this one. It's terrible.

Our cruise ship departing Tampa and crossing under the Sunshine Skyway Bridge.

Our ship docked in Key West, Florida

Ernest Hemingway's House
Key West, Florida

Pretty bird at the Key West Butterfly and Nature Conservatory

Chapter 3

Land Ho!

Funchal in Madeira, Portugal

Tuesday, April 26

I woke up before first light to catch the island all lit up in the early morning as the ship neared the island. By the time Lisa arrived on deck nine, we were both able to witness the sunrise coming up over the island together, it was beautiful. Seeing land was like Christmas morning, we can't wait to step foot on something solid. As we pulled into port, we witnessed Portuguese fishermen returning from the sea with the deck full of the night's haul. It was oh so picturesque!

The marina in Funchal contains a working replica of the Santa Maria, you know from history class, the Nina, Pinta, and . . . yeah, that one. Almost all the buildings in the city were capped with orange terra cotta roofs; there's a real Mediterranean feel here.

Clouds hung over the tops of the huge mountains, draping them most of the day. It caused the weather to be damp and cold, then damp and warm, and then damp and cold again. We had to change into a few dry shirts today. Funchal weather was just preparing us for Paris, ugh!

I didn't have too high an expectation for Funchal, a Portuguese island, but I was pleasantly surprised. Beautiful, clean, and safe, the people were friendly and didn't hawk too much. Lis and I chose to walk from the ship to town, about a ten-minute walk out from the port. We could have grabbed a cab for a one mile ride to town, but we really needed the exercise. We weren't alone on our walk, more than half the ship followed us.

Lisa loved the black and white cobblestone streets with mosaic patterns, they add a lot of interest for pictures. The market in the middle of town had the aroma of fresh fruit in the air. The market also sold island grown fruit like orange, banana, and pineapple. The fruit vender let us try all of them, so we bought two pomegranates to snack on later.

We continued through town along the coast to the Fortaleza de Sao Tiago. It's a historic bright yellow fort with blue boats along the coast just screaming to have their picture taken. Some of the historic alleyways along the way had creative art decorating the walls and doors, some were 3D and skillfully done.

We found a quaint pizza shop near the cable car terminal and ordered prosciutto pizza with a beer. After about ten minutes into our lunch, a young man came by, pulled out his guitar, and played nice soft velvety music. This was officially our first European "moment". Most of our "moments" on this trip came with music, but not all, you'll see.

After finishing lunch, we noticed an empty line for the cable car up the mountain. Motivated by my contempt for lines, we sprung into action and jumped in a car with Janet, a chatty young gal from Minneapolis who traveled by herself. The cable car ride up took our breath away. There were terraced gardens, buildings tucked into the hillside, a tall bridge spanning two mountains, the turquoise ocean, and our cruise ship below.

The end of the cable car ride stopped in the town of Monte halfway up the mountain. We exited the car to explore. The local drivers in Funchal were a somewhat daring lot, speeding along the narrow roads, and sometimes getting a little too close to us pedestrians.

We came upon some adolescent school boys playing futbol at recess. These kids were just what I expected from European futbol players. Extremely skillful and crafty. Watching the artfulness of those young soccer players was a real treat. I'm sure these boys are fantasizing playing like Funchal's own hometown hero, Christian Ronaldo, one of soccer's biggest superstars.

After about a ten minute walk, we stumbled upon Funchal's most iconic tourist attraction. Local men, dressed in traditional garb, steer greased wicker toboggans with their feet, navigating tourists down the 1.2 mile windy mountain roads into town.

Drivers and exhilarated tourists weave their way down the hairpin turns as they've done for over 160 years.

With two hours before departure, we headed back down the cable car into town. We strolled along the ocean walk and admired this elegant old town and marina. We'd amble a little, rest and admire our surroundings, then walk again till we ended back at the docks.

Up the gangplank, through security, and across to our room to freshen up and grab a couple pain pills. We are completely sore from head to toe from all the hills and walking on cobblestones.

When we walked into the Windjammer, we ran into John and Nadia. He's from Tampa, she's from Hungary. After talking with the two of them, I nicknamed Nadia, "Natasha", because her thick Hungarian accent reminds me of an evil character from a James Bond movie. She liked it, so the name stuck. We also found out, they placed all their belongings in storage and decided to do some traveling. Their lease expired and couldn't move into the new place for three weeks, so they decided to travel, like us.

We finally located a hot tub which was actually hot this time of day, but it was crowded, so we floated in the swimming pool to ease our battered bodies, ahhhhh! It was fun being in the pool when the ship was under way - it became a wave pool, moving us around like driftwood.

Day at Sea and Go Through Straight of Gibraltar
Wednesday, April 27

Basically we slept all day and tried to rest up for our big day tomorrow in Malaga, Spain. We took a two hour power nap after breakfast, and a two hour catnap before lunch to recoup from yesterday's excursion. Unfortunately Lisa is still coughing. We are both zonked from all the walking in Funchal, although it was certainly a day to remember.

We ate dinner together on the other side of the dining room behind a room divider with fake plants. Our strategy was to get a break from the "more than slightly annoying" Indian server, he's really overdoing it. When he sees us, it's like a light goes on and he's on us before we sit down, and always overstays his welcome.

I'm still not eating as much from the stomach bug, but Lis thinks she's gaining weight from all the good food, and the food was good.

On the other side of the coin, we really enjoy talking with the young Chinese crew at the meals. They don't seem to have an agenda, and we're fond of their company. Joy and her countrymen seem genuine, just nice innocent kids. They enjoy practicing their English with us and appreciate it. They giggled as I taught them a little slang and told them not to use it with passengers or their bosses.

Tonight we go through the Straight of Gibraltar: Europe on one side, Africa on the other, this is one for the books. Unfortunately passing is at 2 am, and I'm not a night owl, and Lis is still sick. We decided to throw caution to the wind and go for it, we will never get this chance again? It's going to be a late night, no 9 o'clock bedtime for me tonight.

At 11:30 pm we walked up to deck 10 where we could see the lights of Morocco a few miles off on our right. As we moved through the straights, we waved through the open windows to fishermen in rowboats alongside our ship. They had flashlights, so we could see them waving back to us in the dark. One of the Moroccan guys yelled out to us, "Bon Voyage!" It was surreal, a memorable moment, with no music?

Morocco was hilly, and one of the larger hills was covered in huge arabic letters in lights. Morocco sat about two miles to our right and Spain five miles to our left, so Morocco was more our focus. There were only a few lights working on the Spanish coast, so there was less to look at.

At around 2am, the city lights from a distant town silhouetted the mountains of Morocco, the landscape glowed. As we cruise on, an otherworldly orange moon peeked out from the night clouds. It was a mystical scene, almost ominous, and our second magical "moment". This was worth the lost sleep.

We lingered up on deck 10 until 2 am watching the lights and scenes with about 150 fellow passengers. It was a regular "Straights of Gibraltar" crossing party. John and "Natasha" were there, showing off photos of their Funchal open air jeep tour. We have a lot in common with them, both being vagabonds, and the love of travel. Natasha even considered living on a sailboat. I romanticized about that myself, but never too seriously. We couldn't see the Rock of Gibraltar, perhaps too late at night. I guess, it may be much further away, I don't know. With only 3.5 hrs sleep, we woke up at 6 am for Malaga, Spain!

Malaga, Spain

Thursday, April 28

Docked into Malaga, Spain and off the ship, we both agreed to "take it easy today" and "savor the local culture", since Lis was trying to get over this stupid cold. While taking a nice easy stroll through the city and savoring the culture, we came upon a castle named Castillo de Alcazaba. I said to Lis, "It can't be that hard to climb, it's right there, not more than three stories up." Welllllll, there was a bit of an optical illusion going on here. We climbed the first path heading up the mountain. However, we somehow missed a left turn for the lower castle and accidentally headed right for the much HIGHER, Castillo Gilbralfraro.

Dear Lord, it feels like we were going up Mount Kilimanjaro, our muscles are screaming, only pride carried us up from here. Some parts of this path were so steep, even the goats were panting. We'd stop about every ten minutes to prevent ourselves from passing out and to chat with some of the old timers bringing up the rear. Sometimes I'd get a smile from a fellow old geezer as if to say, keep going, you can make it, brother. In all, it took us ninety minutes to the top. So much for taking it easy today. When we finally reached the summit, we discovered a bevy of well-rested, relaxed tourists lounging about who had wisely taken the air-conditioned bus to the summit, egh!

This was one of those "moments" in life we will laugh about later, it was quite the physical accomplishment for us, but right now, we are in pain. After this amazing accomplishment, at least the president of Spain would be at the summit to hand out gold medals, but he wasn't.

The views of the old city and harbor were of course spectacular, and our massive cruise ship looked like a toy in the distance. This old town has an old romantic feel.

We enjoyed a respite and coffee at the little cafe on top of the mountain, time to soak it in. Lis pounded down a lemon beer, which she really enjoyed. From where she sat, her long distance views were to die for. I got stuck looking at her the whole time.

There was a busload of kids at the top for a school trip. The kids were really cute, some of them already posing for the selfies and giggling. The museum next to the cafe wasn't much to talk about. We were probably too exhausted and brain dead to process anything anyway.

After descending from Mt. Olympus, we decided to skip the original castle and aim for the massive old church in town, the

Cathedral de Malaga. We proceeded through the narrow pedestrian streets and came to the old church. "How come I never heard of this church, it's massive?" It probably has its own zip code!

As we were walking through the church, our young protégés from the cruise showed up, John and Natasha, the travel divas, and they shamed us into going back up the small hill to the palace castle which we skipped earlier. So we hung our heads in shame and sheepishly headed back to the palace.

The palace was just OK, plus it involved quite a few more steps, energy we just didn't have to spare, so all in all, egh? After the palace, we walked down the narrow streets we passed through earlier in the day. We found a local watering hole from the 1800's and enjoyed the local beer and tapas.

While we sat at the outside cafe, we were entertained by an old professional gypsy beggar lady going from table to table. She put on such a tremendous fake show of anguish and grief I almost applauded. For act II, a really dark North African lady paraded down the street, balancing an enormous bowl of hand carved animals on her head. She wore a beautiful native dress and was quite the picture. When Lisa took the African lady's photo, she made a beeline to our table and "encouraged" us to buy one of her cumbersome carvings to lug around Europe for the next three months. We passed on her heavy door stoppers, and she went away in a huff.

In pain, stiff and exhausted, we hopped a cab back to the ship. The name of the game now is to get to the pool and hot tub

ASAP. Every bone and joint hurt from the International Goat Olympics. We grabbed our gear, hobbled to the hot tub, and floated in the pool for about a half hour till the ole pirates cleared the deck so we could go in. It's funny, you can be on a ship for two weeks and still not see everyone. Just before the last day of the cruise, a lady walked a dog right in front of me. I haven't seen a dog on this ship before?

Cartagena, Spain
Friday, April 29

Friday we docked in Cartagena, southern Spain, and it was cold, rainy and DAMP. It was a real crappy day to do any exploring, so we bundled up and walked to the middle of town, looked around for a few minutes, gave up and walked back to the ship. It appeared that most passengers never left the ship that day because of the weather.

Not feeling motivated due to the horrible damp cold, we ate lunch, and crashed in the room. If we lived in a northern climate this cold might not be a problem, but we're from the tropics, and this weather sucks. Little did we know these conditions would be the norm for Paris, even into mid June. We've been doing a lot more walking on every excursion, and my dogs are starting to howl.

We said our good-bye to the young Chinese kids, and wished them the best of luck. We will remember them fondly.

Fresh fruit at the local market
Funchal, Madeira, Portugal

In the city of Funchal, on the island of Madeira, Portugal, a cable car takes you
halfway up the mountain. You can see our ship in the distance.

Local men give tourists basket rides down the mountain road.
Funchal, Madeira

In Malaga, Spain we climbed this mountain to see Castillo Gilbralfraro.
The lower castle, Castillo de Alcazaba, is in the distance.

Beautiful pedestrian street near the cathedral
Malaga, Spain

Inside the Cathedral de Malaga
Malaga, Spain

Castillo de Alcazaba, the lower castle on the hill
Malaga, Spain

Pedestrian street where we ate outside at a tapas cafe.
Malaga, Spain

Chapter 4

We're on Our Own

Cruise Ends, Arrive in Barcelona, Spain
Saturday, April 30

The end of the cruise felt like the last day of high school. The ship docked in Barcelona, and we were welcomed with rain, clouds, and yuck. We hung around one of the theaters with our luggage till our names were called. After disembarkation, we waited in a long line in the rain to catch a taxi to our hotel. Thankfully, Lis brought an umbrella!

The Hotel Jardin is in the Gothic section of town next to a historic cathedral which rang its bells every hour till 8 pm. Our gnarly-handed lady cabbie dropped us off as close as she could without driving down a narrow alley, so we walked in the rain from "The Ramblas" to our hotel.

We walked up to the second floor, which in Europe is the first floor, so we walked up one floor to the first floor, get it? We were too early to check-in, so I plugged in the computer and finished our daily update to family and friends. (This is the genesis of the book.)

We hung out and ate lunch in the small upstairs first floor tiny cafeteria a couple hours until our room was ready. Lis and I took the time to rest, dry out, and catch up on the computer; remember two whole weeks without internet. When the sun finally came out, we hustled outside. There were so many beautiful old buildings, we were overwhelmed. We walked into an old church, and mass was going on in Polish . . . wait a minute, Polish, where the hell are we? After a quick go around, we left mass and wandered through the streets. Man, the musicians and singers on the street are better than the paid entertainment on the cruise, *American Idol*, and *The Voice* put together. It was a real treat.

The Ramblas was tourist central, it buzzed with the vibrancy of a beehive: people hopped up on caffeine, hawkers selling trinkets, sidewalk cafes, and my favorite, the monster statue people. The statue people were creative individuals who were all decked out in monster costumes, usually with small stilts to make them look taller. They would pose as still as statues till you approached them, and then startle you if needed. The tradition is, if you posed with them for a picture, you would be expected to give a donation. The living statues were Hollywood quality.

My ankle was swollen, and my knee felt like a sewing needle was jammed into the center of it. I almost fell from the pain a few times, I'm getting old. I wobbled forever to find a place to eat. The trendy restaurants were packed, and the one quiet place we fancied, the waiters never came to take our order, so we left hungry. This will be a frustrating pattern all throughout our European experience.

The walls at the Hotel Jardin were paper thin, so we were forced to listen to an entire herd of young tourist girls chatting it up in their room till midnight. As much as Lis loves chatting it up with the ladies, staying up this late didn't do anything to help her cold and cough.

Tour La Sagrada Familia in Barcelona
Sunday, May 1

We slept in to recover from the move, cruise, mountain climbing, sickness, and time changes. With our backsides dragging, we started out late to the crown jewel of Barcelona, the famous La Sagrada Familia.

With a beautiful day in the forecast, we took the subway green line from the Ramblas, to the blue line for two stops to the grand old La Sagrada Familia, all in about twenty minutes. Upon our arrival, we climbed out of the subway netherworld, into the fresh air and sunlight, and as we turned around our mouths dropped open and shoulders drooped at the sight of this incredible basilica; she was simply breathtaking.

What a sight, we don't have this grandeur in Florida. There were about two thousand tourists outside wandering about, a thousand in line, and God knows how many inside. Only those "special people" who made a reservation a month in advance could get in, it was like visiting the queen. Lis took about two million pictures of the facade, what a work of art!

The Sagrada Familia is a "gihunormous" basilica in the middle of Barcelona. Construction started in 1882, but the architect, Antoni Gaudi, died before it was a quarter finished. The style is a hybrid of Gothic, Curvilinear, and Art Nouveau. It reminds me of wet sand poured in one spot until it forms a peak. It is one crazy beautiful building. If you can't get inside, gaze at the outside for a few hours, it was a bon dia!!!! (Catalan for good day)

After a few hours, we hopped back on the subway again in reverse, we're getting good at this city living stuff. We headed back to the Ramblas for dinner only to find out most everything was closed on Sundays. We walked and walked only to find a Tapas restaurant which was serving diners. They sat us pretty quickly (miracle), and the waiter asked for our drink order. We asked for the local Catalan beer.

After giving our food order and sitting for about fifteen minutes, I waved the waiter over to ask for our drinks before the meal. He motioned with his hands and nodded as if to say he'd be right there. He then proceeded to ignore us for another fifteen minutes. He passed by me another five times, never even making eye contact. There were even times he appeared to have nothing to do. I reached my boiling point, I've had enough. I grabbed my jacket and stormed out the door. This guy must have seen me starting to get up, so he gathered our drinks as we walked past him on the way out the door. He held my beer looking as if to say, "Is there something wrong?" "%$# you!" This is what you get when waiters don't work for tips. I was steaming! We will not be visiting many restaurants in Europe where you are at the mercy of servers.

Starving and about to punch someone, we headed back to the Ramblas, the main tourist stroll in the Gothic region where we found a Middle Eastern restaurant serving lamb shish kabob with the ever illusive, timely service. Two meals in Spain so far is an exercise in extreme patience. It's no wonder everyone here is so skinny, and they are.

Exhausted physically and emotionally, we walked home and pre-packed for tomorrow. After falling asleep, we were awoken by a couple of young well-oiled revelers stumbling down our street at 4:30 am. Even with some of the sketchy things which happened to us, Barcelona was still a beautiful vibrant town with lots more to see. I really wished we would have stayed longer than two nights.

Flight from Barcelona to Nice, Train to Antibes for Two Nights
Monday, May 2

Woke up at 5 am, showered, and waited for the taxi our hotel so kindly procured. The taxi picked us up right in front of the hotel, and as we left, we navigated through the extremely narrow alleys on to the streets and off to the airport (€41). At the Barcelona International Airport, we boarded a jam packed Easy Jet and off to Nice. All the arrangements for this flight were done online.

On our way to Nice, we flew over the majestic snow-capped Pyrenees mountains, across southern France, and eventually arriving in Nice. Our flight was just ahead of another full plane from Moscow, Russia. Our plane emptied into the airport terminal, followed right behind by a crowd of Russian passengers, and we all bottlenecked in customs. The two man, less than energetic operation took about forty-five minutes. Our solitary suitcases were the last to be picked up because we made a Water Closet stop, and the entire Russian plane got ahead of us.

Bathroom Report: Normal, nothing to see here, folks.

Right outside of customs, we purchased our tickets, waited fifteen minutes and boarded the bus to Antibes. Yeah, we're in France traveling the Cote d' Azure (Blue Coast), along the Mediterranean, we are in la la land. The towns along the way looked like normal American seaside towns, but as we closed in on

Antibes, we were disappointed with the amount of graffiti on the old buildings, noise barriers, and trains. This wasn't on the tourist brochures?

When we entered Antibes proper, with our brains in a fog, we had no idea where we were to get off in town, so we made an uneducated guess. We passed a sign a mile back for "Hotel Astor" (our hotel), but it couldn't have been it. Ours was on top of a big hill, and we were at sea level? We pushed the "Arret" button, the bus stopped, and we disembarked. Luggage in hand, no detailed map, can't speak the language, and totally lost.

Being disoriented and my French being pedestrian at best, we approached a local young mother with stroller, "Parle vous English?" Her facial expressions implied, "Not really, but I'll help." "Ou est?" as I handed her the address. This lovely young mother stayed with us for about 15 minutes, searched her smartphone and pointed out the correct direction we should walk to our hotel. She was our first introduction to some lovely French hospitality.

Walking about twenty minutes and up a steep two block hill in a residential area, we finally arrived to our Hippy Mountaintop Hotel Astor. I call it the Hippy Hotel because the office window has a large peace sign. Yes, it was the same Hotel Astor we had passed a mile back. The sign on the flat road led to a long flight of steps up a steep hill to the HMHA.

Meeting us at the iron gates, JC, the awesome French owner, welcomed us in near perfect English and filled us in on our local surroundings and the workings of the apartment. The hotel walls were adorned with positive message posters. Hand painted river rocks, personalized by previous tenants, decorated many a flat surface. These "good vibes" are just what the doctor ordered!

Our room was large for European standards with a king-sized bed, TV, private bathroom, and separate galley kitchen with everything we'd need for our stay. The cozy little balcony peered over the roofs of the surrounding homes, and the small table chairs were perfect for morning coffee.

We were totally exhausted, so we unpacked and laid down for a short nap before we hit the streets of Antibes. However, we didn't wake up until the next day. Because Lis was still sick and lacking energy, she stayed home. I headed out to explore solo, on my aching feet and sore knees. Moving towards town, I did my best to memorize all the turns and landmarks for my eventual return home. I don't speak the language very well, had no phone, and didn't even have a detailed map of the area, so the pressure's on, I better remember my way home.

Making my way through town, I turned and headed toward the sea. As I approached the retaining wall, something caught my attention out of the corner of my eye. An imposing old fortress stood right there, in the middle of this modern town. I poked around the outside of this Musée d'Archéologie citadel for a while, then continued along the picturesque ocean road toward Picasso's museum.

*Bathroom Report: Nice looking stand alone building in the park by the sea, but filthy inside, with graffiti and no door on the stall. The men's urinal had an opening in the wall at eye level for a view. The inside filth was a little strange, because the city is so upscale?

So many of the historic alleys in this beautiful town are a framable picture. I observed two couples walking with purpose down one of these alleys, and followed them thirty feet, and down three flights of steps to an outdoor marché (market). The marché was pretty foreign to me, everything in French, weights in kilos. Reading French and listening to it are two different worlds. I wandered around like an alien in a strange planet. The Tapenade monger allowed me to taste his olive paste on a cracker, and it was Y.U.M.M.Y., so I bought some.

Some differences with Europe and the U.S. when it comes to groceries: loose perishables are sold by the kilo, so you must figure out how many kilograms you want, and ask for it in French. One kilo equals 2.21 pounds, or 1 pound equals .45 kilograms, etc. I would just round up to cinquante (50).

I don't know about the rest of Europe, but France uses a comma instead of a dot when writing currency. Example: 2,50 which amounts to two and a half euros. They also use a dot where in the U.S. we use a comma, for example: 1.000 for one thousand. The number one looks like a 7 with a droopy top, and the number seven has a dash through the middle.

I ran out of my five ounces of travel water an hour ago, and am dying of thirst, and can't find water. I see lots of restaurants, but no groceries or convenience stores. After what seemed an eternity of walking, I finally found the trendy part of town and a little store which sold "O", which is French for water. Since my Spanish and French were melded together in Barcelona, and my head still in a fog, I forgot how to say "two" in French, but the sweet lady knew what this turkey tried to say, since I was holding up two fingers and mumbling incoherently. She just smiled and nodded. I guzzled the first bottle of O down in two gulps, and all the cells in my body celebrated the beautiful spring rain.

Now starving and looking for a place to eat, I found a small cafe/restaurant which displayed pre-made sandwiches behind a glass. Lucky for me the lady in front of me ordered just what I wanted. I knew the French word for "the same", woo hoo!

"Bonjour, le meme sil vous plait," . . . it worked.

"Mayonnaise?"

"Oui."

He wrapped the baguette au poulete like a Christmas present, handed it to me, and I was on my way! Famished, I found a bench around the corner and polished off the tomato chicken sandwich like a man going to the electric chair, or the guillotine, being where I was.

After lunch, I explored more of the town. My hair felt long, and I could really use a haircut, but all the barber shops were closed. So I made my way home after five hours exploring, and took two pain pills. Every walkway was concrete or wobbly cobblestone, apparently designed to snap your foot off at the ankle. Lis rested all day, hand washed a little laundry, and hung the clothes on a drying rack on the balcony. When I arrived home, she took the XX strength cough medicine I purchased at the blinking green sign pharmacy place.

Later in the evening, I summoned the strength to walk downhill to the grocery, and picked up some sliced deli meat, steak fries, milk, coffee, baguette, wine, sugar, and two servings of hot Ratatouille. I didn't know what Ratatouille was, but I watched the movie, and had to try it.

There were few products I recognized, and all labeling was in French. This would be our best meal since leaving the ship. Oh, by the way, I LOVED Antibes and wished we stayed there a few more days. Resting in bed, Lis didn't get to see Antibes at all, poor thing!

Pedestrian street in the Gothic section
Barcelona, Spain

La Sagrada Familia
Barcelona, Spain

Sea Wall near Picasso Museum
Antibes, France

Marina
Antibes, southern France

City street near the Mediterranean Sea
Antibes, France

Chapter 5

It's Nice in Nice

Train from Antibes to Nice

Wednesday, May 4

The next day we finished packing, squishing all of our clothes into those travel vacuum bags so everything could fit. As a courtesy, JC drove us to the train station and dropped us off. After we arrived, Lis used the ticket window again because we couldn't figure out another ticket machine. Not all the ticket machines have an "English" option, so it can be really frustrating.

While waiting on the train station platform, we realized just in time we were on the wrong side of the tracks (my life story). Panicked, we hustled to carry our Buick-sized luggage down steps to an underground tunnel for the other side. Two kind young men and two teenage femmes offered to help us with our heavy luggage.

We smiled and thanked them, but politely declined. When the train arrived and while Lis struggled to climb onto the train, the two "nice fellas" jammed up behind her, lifted her travel bag and opened the zipper. When the creeps saw me see them, I yelled, and they ran like the wind. Gypsy scum!

The local trains along the Cote d'Azure have "quiet" cars, which is the type we found ourselves on. While we sat face to face with a young college student studying for school, a not so quiet passenger was prattling loudly on the phone right behind her. The college student, who seemed to be getting flustered by the racket, ever so gently turned and educated this uninformed passenger of this train's quiet policy and her present location. Ms. Nobody-is-going-to-tell-me-to-be-quiet lady was offended at the young student's revelations and fought like the devil she was in the right. The college student stayed reserved but persistent, and finally Ms. Nobody-is-going-to-tell-me-to-be-quiet lady understood the error of her ways, or her call ended. She hung up the phone, and finally closed her fat obnoxious pie hole. Victory for the sweet girl!

When we arrived at the Niceville station, center city Nice, we now needed to purchase tickets for the above ground Tram for the next leg of our journey. Finding the right ticket machine was hard enough, but we had to figure out a new machine without an English option. We smashed our head against the ticket machine hoping that would help, but it didn't.

We were running out of options. It did take credit card and coins, but not paper currency. So together we scrounged up just enough loose coins to purchase two €1,50 tickets just to get us to our new home base apartment. After our close encounter with pickpockets back at the Antibes train station, we are hyper vigilant trying to spot out any scurvy dogs. I spotted a couple shady blokes hanging out by the exit doors that might be trouble. I'll keep an eye on them.

A half block from the train station is the street tram to Acropolis. We hopped on, luggage in tow for five stops. It's a little embarrassing lugging all this luggage on the tram. I feel like such a tourist. I stumbled out, and followed Colette's translated instructions for the equivalent of two hundred feet from the tram stop to our apartment building.

Finding her building, we rang her apartment at the main entrance outside the lobby door. From her apartment above, she buzzed us into the lobby where we had to squeeze into a mini elevator (I've seen roomier coffins) with all our luggage. We pulled the outer door shut, pressed seven, the inner door closed and up we went, talk about claustrophobic!

Our petit grey haired host greeted us at the door and welcomed us in for tea and snacks at arrival. After tea, Colette walked us around and showed us how to operate all the appliances. Colette would often say "allo" and "voila," an English word or two, followed by a lot more French in-between. Her English was as limited as my French, so I pulled out our mini laptop and used Google Translate to communicate with her. She really got a kick out of it.

Our bedroom was the master inside this two-bedroom 7th floor apartment where Colette lives by herself. Outside our room, we share a clean galley kitchen with our host. Our large bathroom is modern, clean, and private.

The shared galley kitchen was traditional, with a large refrigerator, coffee maker, microwave, toaster, 220 volt quick water boiler, regular stove top, and clothes washer under the counter we were allowed to use.

After getting acclimated, we took a stroll down to the Old Town to the famous Promenade of the English. While walking past the marina, we decided to spy out the yachts of the empathy-challenged super-rich and their sycophantic tourist fan club.

There were eight super yachts lined up according to price in descending order, all trying to outdo each other. It was actually pretty nauseating. Away from these small fry millionaires and over to where cruise ships park, we spotted the "Octopus", George Allen's opulent city on the water yacht. This imposing behemoth has not one but two helicopter pads with two helicopters, two submarine bays with two submarines (you can't just have one), and a yacht-sized dingy with its own dingy, go figure. George is co-owner of Microsoft.

The weather was lovely, so we walked along the ocean so Lis could take pictures of the beautiful landscapes and buildings. We continued along the Promenade des Anglais for about a mile till we reached La Petit Train kiosk in front of the famous Hotel Negresco.

Nice doesn't have sand like Florida or New Jersey, no, no, that would be American. They have rocks, big ones, many as large as your fist. You have to wear some type of durable shoes in order to stagger onto this beach. It's amazing to see people laying on rocks with just a towel under them.

Now that we're not carrying luggage and under pickpocket pressure, we'll stop at a tram platform to attempt to figure out those ticket machines. Not rushed and with a little time and patience, viola, we figured it out. You have to really push your credit card deep into the slot just to get the ball rolling. Yeah, we finally have our ten trip tickets for €10.

Up to Èze
Saturday, May 7

Early morning light is best for pictures, so we're off to the bus station before sunrise, headed east for Èze. Colette pointed out the Vauban bus station from the 7th floor balcony, but when we got to street level we were discombobulated as to how to get there. We eventually got our bearings and made it down to the bus station with a half hour to spare.

This bus is part of the local system, so it only cost one ticket each (€1 if you buy the pack of ten). When the bus came, we ended up sitting across from a Korean mother and son who reminded us of our old neighbors from many years ago.

Up and around, up and around, the views were spectacular and just a smidgen terrifying navigating the steep cliffs. We passed above the picturesque town of Ville de France, a stop Colette insisted we see. It's a scenic old ocean town with cute little shops and the Rothschild museum.

Èze sits on the top of a mountain, but the bus drops you off at the bottom of the city. From there, you have to walk up and around to see this quaint little gem. We knew before we left for Europe we would be doing a lot of walking, so we exercised for months before we left and bought new walking shoes.

We found and used the bathroom before our trek up into town, and then made our way up the mountain. Bathroom Report: By the Tourist Information (TI) office just off the road, this WC had a ticket window with a cashier to take your €.50 or to give change. La toilette was "normal" aside from the cash register.

Èze is a small, historical, pedestrian-only village on the way to Monaco from Nice. It has oodles of cute little alleyways with stone buildings and grottos which housed trendy little shops. The town is loaded with character. Lis loves the antique doors, windows and flowers for pictures. If you look past the touristy commercialism, you see the old layout and tiny dwellings of the former inhabitants.

At the peak of the village is a well-maintained cactus garden with benches and weathered statues of young, slender ladies. From the garden, you have long-distance views of the villages below and miles of the blue Mediterranean waters.   It was absolutely stunning!!

We paid €6 each to enter the fancy cactus garden portion of the city.   Although the garden itself wasn't much to look at, the long-distance views were "you've got to be kidding me" beautiful. Pictures of the view and words just can't describe what we're seeing. You can see for about 100 miles across the Mediterranean on a clear day, with a great view of Papaya beach. Èze was one of our favorite places on the whole trip. :-)

On the way home from Èze, the bus driver must have had a date, because we were flying down the mountain.   Lisa decided "we" now want to see the Russian Orthodox Church in Nice. Earlier when she planned for all day in Èze, she decided "we" didn't want to see the Russian Church today, but now "we" do. We exited our bus back at Vauban, hopped on the Tram to Niceville, and walked the rest of the way through town to the church.

This orthodox church was built in 1912 for the growing number of Russian visitors to Nice, and was paid for by Czar Nicholas II right before he was murdered by the Bolsheviks. It was the most beautifully maintained church I've ever seen. I've seen lots of "gihunormous" old churches, but this looks like they finished it yesterday with the best of materials, and Rubles were not a problem.

We are really getting the hang of this public transportation, and I'm picking up enough French to eavesdrop on people's conversations. :) By the way, according to a couple of young college girls on the bus to Èze, we found out there was an awesome party last night at the college with immature English boys who spoke French way too loud.

We needed real food, so Colette told us where her super marché was. I ventured down the block expecting an old-fashioned French 'Mom and Pop' marché with Mister wearing a horizontally-striped black and white shirt, red beret, while playing an accordion. Instead, it was a Carrefour, similar to a French Walmart.

After shopping for about twenty minutes, the lines to pay were very long, slow, and confusing, so I left the cart and walked home hungry. Back to Colette's for crackers and cheese dinner, topped off with a bottle of a 2013 Bordeaux.

With the promise of sketchy weather for the next two days, we decided to take it easy on Sunday. Ninety percent of everything is closed anyway, and busses run less frequently. Desiring to stay local, we walked five minutes to the iconic seven-story blockhead library building at the Acropolis. The "block" portion of the building is four stories, and has a working space inside the head. It was the first "inhabitable sculpture" and was great for black and white "artistic pictures".

After Blockhead, we jumped the tram to the famous Place de Masséna, the center square where white glass male statues sit atop ten-foot poles. Along with great people-watching, we enjoyed the yummy vanilla ice cream and listened to some relaxing street performer classical music. This would be considered another "moment".

Riding the public transportation here can be a study in boundary toleration and personal spaces. It can be really cozy sometimes. Someone once said that life begins right outside your comfort zone; well, we're right outside now. I am definitely a country person, though this city experience has been quite enriching!

St. Paul de Vence and Public Toilets
Monday, May 9

We got a good night's sleep last night and are ready to hit it hard. We rose early, and Colette had la petit dejeuner ready for us on the balcony. Since our apartment was in town, our view overlooked the city. The view was still lovely, with all the rooftop gardens, family cats stalking the pigeons, and tall mountains in the distance surrounding the city.

For breakfast, Colette always serves coffee, tea, baguettes, butter, jam, yogurt, pastry, nuts and fruit on bone china. Her attention to detail was meticulous; she thought of everything. After breakfast, it's out the door, down the coffin-sized elevator, and up the street for the tram to Place Masséna, where we walked to the Verdun bus station.

The bus ride from Nice to St. Paul de Vence was about an hour, and for some reason, we are starting to see a trend here; the

French don't seem to consider fresh air circulation high on their priority list. It was uncomfortably stuffy on the bus.

To clear-up an awful stereotype, 99% of the French people we smelt, smelt just fine. Except for this one young fella standing by the tram today, thank God we were outside.

The inner city of Nice where we stayed, away from the billionaire yachts at the marina, is a normal, active city with quite a diversity of people. Office workers, construction workers, professionals, and students go about their business and call this town home.

We arrived at St. Paul de Vence around 11:00 am. It's an old medieval fortress town with its original walls, yes of course up a mountain (it's always up a damn mountain). Several famous artists resided and worked here, including Marc Chagall who lived out his final years and is buried right outside the ancient city walls.

Saint Paul was lovely, but like Èze, it was commercialized. It wasn't tacky, but with very expensive, trendy art shops, et al. Total cost of the day for the bus transport, food, and bathrooms: €5, all because we packed our lunch.

Lisa took about three million pictures there; every step you take is another priceless photo, and if you turn around there's another one, ooh la la! Little ancient alleyways with handcrafted mosaic walkways, old doors brimming with time-honored character, hanging potted plants and stone walls everywhere, just gorgeous. From the top of the original walls, you have amazing long-distance views of houses on the distant hillside with cloud-covered mountains in the background.

Weather in May when we were there is a bit like Pennsylvania in March. If you wait long enough, you'll experience all four seasons in one day (except it's always damp). I could never get used to cold and damp. Cold yes, damp yes, but never the two together.

Bathroom Report: Every trip to a public toilette is an adventure: some don't have seats, and most cost money, usually .50 euro. Today the bus dropped us off at St. Paul, right in front of the big stand-alone stainless steel bathroom. I needed to change my sweaty shirt from the stuffy bus ride and use the little boys' room. When I started to change my shirt, the toilet seat started to shut on its own, like a horror movie, and it dawned on me, "Oh crap, this might been one of those 'self-cleaning' bathrooms I heard of." I didn't know if it would wait for me to get out. Not quite getting my shirt all the way down, I got out tout de suite. If you're wondering, yes, it was a self-cleaner, and it did wait till after I left. We stood outside afterwards listening, and it sounded like a washing machine inside. When Lis walked in after me, everything was wet: toilet, floor, sink, like someone took a shower.

Bonus Bathroom Report #2 for the day: After about two hours of sightseeing and drinking all our travel water, I discovered another tiny public restroom tucked away in the middle of town. Sometimes you just have to take advantage of these rare bathroom sightings. I stepped into this skinny, dark hallway about 2' x 6' with a stainless-steel trough, with only a 6" wide "privacy" wall between the attendee and the viewing public outside. Also for the viewing public, no door was provided, and the ladies room was right opposite the men's trough. If a lady wanted to go to her closet type room (for .20 euro, dudes were free) she'd almost have to bump the male occupant WHILE he was doing his tinkle. Fortunately for everyone, no one else needed to go while I was there. I got out of there tout de suite.

We took the circuit bus back to Hotel Negresco and sauntered down the Promenade along the ocean toward the marina till we got home. Hungry, we picked up food at Carrefour, and this time hung in there all the way to the cashiers. We purchased sushi, cooked chicken, cheese, and nuts. Your friendly cashier can and will rummage through any bags you brought into the store. I guess a lot of people use the old five-finger discounts in these parts?

OK, a French lesson for today: if your bill comes out to anything and 99 cents, for 99 cents the French say, "Four twenties, nineteen," quatre-vingt-dix-neuf, so you better be quick and have a calculator. We're not advanced in the language, I'm still counting on my fingers, so we just looked at the monitor above the cash register.

We're ignorant of proper European elevator etiquette, they are so small only three French people or one and a half normal Americans could fit inside one comfortably. When we returned home from Carrefour, a young lady was waiting at the lobby lift, and since we don't know the etiquette, we tentatively got on with the now semi-terrified young lady.

After the elevator door shut, she quizzed me in FRENCH, "Quel etage?" Oh shit, I panicked, how do you say seven in French, no time to start counting with my fingers. I panicked, "Sank," which is five. Damn, we needed seven, which is "sept"! How am I going to get out of this predicament with some dignity? The lift stopped, the young lady got off at the 4th floor with a smile and an "Au revoir." So after the door shut, I pressed "sept", and we were home free, sounding like a local.

Castle Hill Fortress and Cemetery in Nice
Tuesday, May 10

These continental breakfasts just aren't cutting it. I was really hankering for eggs for breakfast, and I know there is a McDonald's three blocks away near Carrefour. Early, before breakfast, I scurried down the street four blocks only to find out McDonald's DOESN'T OPEN TILL 9 am, WHAT? Only five days in France and we have found one restaurant whose kitchen was closed for lunch, another whose fritie (french fries) machine broke, another ran out of chicken, and now a world-famous franchised breakfast restaurant closed for most of breakfast. Sacre bleu!! No wonder everyone here is so thin!!!!???

We decided not to go to Ville le France because of the high chance of rain, so we walked to the marina where the super yachts dock. Feeling confident, we decided to go on to conquer Castle Hill, another mountain fortress. I wish we could find forts which go downhill. From ground level, it appeared to be about three stories up, so what the heck, let's do it. Well, it turned out this expedition had multiple levels beyond the three-story vista you see from the ground level. At every level we were treated with a new visual surprise and a temptation to move onward and upward. We discovered waterfalls halfway up, Roman ruins at the summit, and a great cemetery.

After trudging all the way up, we found out once more a paved road leading to a mountaintop cafe. To add insult to injury, the little white train was already there with twenty well-rested tourists enjoying a snack and cold cocktail. After finally conquering this mountain, we were again expecting the president of France to pin a medal on us for our fortress conquering, but it didn't happen. We are, however, getting in better shape.

We were surprised to see a twenty-foot tall waterfall and grotto built halfway up. It was built in 1920 to help attract tourists to Nice, and it's still working. We walked around the splash zone, pointing our umbrella toward the falls to protect ourselves from the spray. The water cascaded down the hill and into the grottos; you could hear splashing the whole way up.

From the top, you could see the city of Nice down below, along the coastline. The terra cotta roofs looked beautiful against the bright aqua water of the Mediterranean, truly stunning! On the opposite side of the mountain from the promenade was the marina with the fancy, colorful boats. We found a bench and ate our packed lunch while looking at the amazing view of the blue water, with the sound of the waves crashing below.

Another surprise at noon was a LOUD cannon firing from who-knows-where. It scared the bejesus out of us tourists. I sat across from a young Korean lady at the time. She looked at me as if to say, what the hell was that? I shrugged my shoulders. The explosion may have come from a fort on another mountain, behind the town. How about giving a brother a "Fire in the hole" before shooting off a friggin cannon? A warning in French would not have helped, because most tourists wouldn't have understood it anyway? But still?

We could have taken the same steps down, which would have been easy and predictable. If we didn't get lost, what would we have to write about, so off we went through the woods following signs for the cemetery Chateau du Nice. Cemeteries are always good for pictures and views, because dead rich people love spectacular views. Lisa and I became separated, and she got lost following bread crumbs left by young German tourists. After about a half hour, we finally met up inside the cemetery, and she was able to get some great pictures.

This was one of the most beautiful cemeteries we've ever seen. It was like a museum with ornate statues, large tombstones, rose bushes, and long-distance views of Nice with mountains in the background. Most of the tombstones and monuments were from Napoleon's time. The cemetery was on different levels of the hillside, so it kept climbing up and up. The statues were so large it was like a sculpture garden. These people here really knew how to die in style.

We worked our way downhill toward Old Town Nice through a bustling market, with all those adorable little shops, street entertainers, and outdoor cafes. The town was laid out similar to the medieval Gothic section of Barcelona, but the buildings here had brighter, happier colors. Many of the locals still hang clothes out on the balcony. It makes for good, colorful pictures.

We picked up the Tram at Place Masséna and headed home. We've really enjoyed this town, so we'll have to add this to our Bucket List so we can cross it off.

Bathroom report: On top of Castle Hill was a rustic free-standing building bathroom. No charge, but not the most modern or cleanest. You get what you pay for, I guess.

Tomorrow we leave Nice and have a four-hour train ride to Arles. Arles sits in the center of windy southern France in the Provence region. The weatherman is calling for rain all day. Hopefully we can stay dry as we walk from the train station in Arles to the B&B. The B&B website states our room is one block away from a restored Roman amphitheater in the center of the old town. We are stoked!

Promenade of the English
Nice, France

Marina with Castle Hill in the distance
Nice, France

89

Street in Old Town, Nice after coming down Castle Hill

Blockhead library administration building, first inhabitable sculpture
Nice, France

Gorgeous pedestrian narrow alley
Èze, France

Courtyard and fountain
Èze, France

Narrow alley with cute little shops
Èze, France

*View of the Mediterranean Sea from the cactus garden of
Èze, France*

*Cemetery where Marc Chagall is buried
St. Paul de Vence, France*

Courtyard fountain
St. Paul de Vence, France

Narrow pedestrian road along the outer walls of
St. Paul de Vence, France

Chapter 6

Dungeon In Arles, France

Train from Nice to Avignon, Bus to Arles

Wednesday, May 11

Said "au revoir" to Colette with the computer playing classic French music and a translated thank-you note on the screen. Colette was touched, she gave Lis the "la bise" (the kiss on the cheek) and a gift-wrapped lavender scented soap, and we headed out for Arles.

We lumbered to the Tram with our 800 pounds of gear. We also carried bread and fruit from our la petit dejeuner (breakfast) to snack on the train.

Arriving at the train station, we had to figure out those yellow ticket machines for the TGV bullet train to Avignon. It took trying three machines, two trips to the info guy, and about a half hour to figure those things out. Good thing we left an hour and a half early for the trip.

The day is damp, rainy, and sometimes chilly. It's the kind of weather, if you dress too warm you sweat, and if you dress too light you freeze. I bet the guys change their shirt two or three times a day here. While waiting at the train station in a wet shirt, I thought, *"I'm not paying €.50 just to change my shirt in the bathroom when I don't have to tinkle."* I found a coin-operated picture booth with a big curtain and voila, in and out with a new dry shirt, oh yeah!

If you need to cross the rails back in the Niceville train station, they have a handy escalator. On this particular trip down the escalators, Lis reached back to rearrange her luggage and was pulled backwards in slow motion by the weight of her backpack. Trapping herself between her luggage and the glass sides of the escalator, she screamed, "Help, I can't get up!" With a smile I grabbed her hand, pulling with all my strength and using the weight of my backpack, returned her normal upright position, just before a near certain death at the bottom of the escalator. This may be why the French don't have too many escalators?

Well, the TGV "bullet train" pulled into the station on time, we boarded, secured our luggage, and got comfortable. Upon moving for a few miles, I thought, *"This is more like a BB gun train, where's the flash?"* The cars are smooth as silk (they weld their rails together here), but the SEPTA train in Philly goes just as fast as this one on open ground.

OK, get this, the first-class cars feel hermetically sealed and don't seem to have any air movement again. When we first arrived on the train, it was somewhat stuffy. It wasn't hot, but very humid and stale air. If this is first class, what's it like in second class?

We started off smooth and slow and passed through Cannes during the famous film festival. Offshore in Cannes, you could see the million and billionaires with their extravagant prized yachts on display within sight in the ocean. My God, most countries don't have navies this big! Our train rode along the coastline, with the Mediterranean Sea sometimes only about fifty feet away from our train. As we continued west, we left the big cities and meandered more into the countryside with lush green vineyards and tree-covered mountains. Red poppies grow wildly here along the roads like weeds, and it's very picturesque.

Many of the houses along the way were tired old stone homes with terra cotta roofs, not the pristine villas I'd expected in Provence. At one point, we caught a glimpse of an enormous Roman aqueduct in the distance. Now you know you're in Europe! Our original intention was to rent a car in Arles and drive to the aqueduct Pont du Guard, but if we don't have time at least we saw one from the train.

When we finally got outside all the little towns and more into the country, our "BB" train conductor hit the gas and WOAH SWEET BABY JESUS we were flying. You could feel down to your bones the incredible acceleration. In the front of our car was a TV screen which tracked our speed, and at times it hit over 300 km/hr

(186 mph). When we'd pass another train going the other way, you'd feel the air pressure drop in the cabin, and swoosh!!!!! It would startle you the first few times, but after about five passes, we got used to it.

When we arrived at the mall-like Avignon train station, we rushed like loons through it and out the back doors to the empty bus stop, and proceeded to wait an hour for our bus. I still don't know why we ran? We could have waited comfortably inside. When our bus arrived, we made ourselves comfortable, and we're on our way. It began to drizzle as we continued, and downpoured along the way till we finally arrived at the Arles (pronounced "Arl") bus station.

Thankfully, the solid downpour our bus drove through slowed down enough for us to walk the fifteen minutes to our B&B without getting totally soaked. Streets here are narrow, sidewalks tiny, and many walk in the streets. When a car speeds by, people dart out of the way of an almost certain death onto the narrow sidewalks. Thankfully our B&B is on a pedestrian street, rarely if ever used by cars.

We walked about a mile with our full kit in the cold rain, and it was miserable cold with a breeze, and you guessed it, Lis got sick (again). We later found out in the middle of this week Arles has a free tourist bus which would have picked us up from the train station and dropped us off one hundred feet from our B&B's front door. It would have been nice if our host would have told us about this wonderful tourist bus. She was aloof and distant, and I soon got the impression she didn't care for bourgeoise Americans.

We are staying with Nicole and Pierre (names changed to protect the guilty). They live in a very small 400 year old, three-story stone home in the old part of Arles, one block from a 2,000-year-old Roman amphitheater. Pierre speaks excellent English since he attended school in England as a child.

Our "room" is on the ground floor of the home. The second floor has the family bedrooms, and the third floor contains the living room and kitchen. The stairway was very steep with random lengths and varying heights in the steps. It was so very awkward and dangerous to climb. The handrail is loose and secured with bubble gum and duct tape. These stairs would never pass any building inspection in the U.S. Because of the stairs and Nicole, we would rarely venture upstairs, even though we had access to the family room and kitchen. Our B&B hosts were getting out of the hospitality business, so they were not too hospitable to their last guest. For breakfast, they'd leave out a bowl and a choice of three cereals and coffee. Sometimes we'd have to wait till he got back from the store with groceries. This breakfast was a far cry from Colette's beautiful arrangement of la petit dejeuner on the terrace balcony.

Our first-floor bedroom had old wooden beams in the ceiling, and the walls were of ancient stone. The king-sized bed had no room to walk around, you had to climb over it from the foot. There was no closet, hangers, or a place to hang clothes. No refrigerator, microwave, or TV. No shelving but for a windowsill you had to clear when you closed the inside shutter for privacy. Lighting was at a premium, as was floor space. Several tiles were loose and clinked or clunked every time you walked on them. Last but not least, the toilet was in the cold, dark lobby also used as a storage room. I can't believe this place received a five star rating?

Our only window looks out from the bedroom at a door across the street in the narrow alley which never gets sunlight. The house across the way has honeysuckle vines growing up the side of the house. The nicest thing in our room is a view of the neighbor's door.

Our room has a lot of character, although it's damp, like a wet Philadelphia basement in winter. There were nights we had to put our sheets in the dryer before going to bed. Nicole, the wife, never gave us any indication we would even have access to heat. For our first day, she let us live in the cold, damp room. When Pierre returned home from work, he showed us how to operate his medieval radiator from hell. The heating system worked well, once it was turned on. Thanks for nothing, Nicole!

We have access to the washing machine and for once a dryer. It was nice for Lisa not having to hand-wash the laundry. The dials and buttons are all in French. We needed help from Pierre from time to time, to figure out the machine settings.

Most appliances here are so much smaller than the U.S., but they appear to last much longer. The washing machine in our B&B appeared to be at least twenty years old. I can only imagine the look on a European's face if they could see how big the average American appliances and homes are. Our appliances may use more energy, but again, we don't have to go to market every day and waste time and gas.

First Full Day Exploring Arles
Thursday, May 12

Thursday started out raining. Pierre informed us there's an unusual cold front visiting the area, egh, so we waited in our little 400-year-old (cold and dank) room till the sun came out around 10:30. We needed to rest from all of yesterday's travel anyway.

When we left our room, turned right down the alley road for another 40 feet, turn right, we are greeted by a gigantic Roman amphitheater whose main steps are but eighty feet away. We couldn't see it from our room because of how close the buildings are to each other. After exploring the arena and taking a gazillion pictures, we toured the Baths of Constantine and inside the well-preserved Church/Abby of Saint Trophime. Constantine II was born here, and Arles was also a retirement city for Rome's VI legion.

I might be coming down with Lisa's cold now, but we're hearing about rain tomorrow, so we pressed on to get some things done.

Everyday people of Arles walk among ancient structures. Some were built over 2000 years ago, and man, a lot of effort went into these things. The amphitheater reminded me of all the sports stadiums I've ever been in, and it was in excellent condition. The amphitheater was built in 90 AD by the Romans for the whole "bread and circus" routine. Years later, it evolved into a small fortress town, and a pilgrimage site for a martyr named Genesius.

Arles Archeology Museum on a Rainy Day
Friday, May 13

I've been sick now, so I'm behind in writing our journal. Rain/cold yesterday, so we just bundled up, occasionally walking around until it would start to rain too hard. Lis and I are still rocking from two weeks at sea. We don't have our land legs yet. Looking for something to do inside, we found the free tourist bus our host never told us about, thanks a lot! We decided to take in the Arles Archeology Museum, a couple miles outside of town. Being inside the museum would be good for this rainy day. The museum was really well put together with preserved artifacts and reconstructions of the former inhabitants, dwellings, river activities, etc. The weather in Arles has been cold and damp, but inside the museum it was cool and dry with normal bathrooms.

Train to Avignon to See Papal Palace and Bridge
Saturday, May 14

Decided yesterday to take the train to Avignon today, due to the favorable weather forecast, sunny and 75 degrees, yes! Avignon is best-known in history as the short-term residence of the French popes during a schism with the Roman Catholic Church in 1309-1377. There is also a famous song from the 16th century every French child learns in school called, "Sur la pont d' Avignon" or "On the Bridge at Avignon". It's a catchy little tune, like Disney's "It's a Small World", a song which can replay in your head for days and drive you mad.

Sur le pont d'Avignon,   *On the bridge of Avignon,*
On y danse, on y danse,   *They dance, dance*
Sur le pont d'Avignon,   *On the bridge of Avignon,*
On y danse, tous en rond.   *We dance all in circles*

We took advantage of the local train from Arles to Avignon, and the train dropped us off right across the street from the entrance to the old city. On the way to the tourist information building, we passed a McDonald's, OMG we are hungry for American food and we NEVER eat at McDonald's (other than the occasional breakfast McMuffin).

We vowed to stop at Micky D's on the way back, a real French experience, eh? Lisa tried to find the bathroom this morning when we entered inside the old town. It took four failed sorties before she eventually found one, inside the Papal Palace. Bathroom report: Normal, free, and the best so far!

The town was clean with an upper middle class feel. We walked the wide pedestrian causeway in-between the many cafes and shops. A couple blocks uphill and around the corner, we discovered the Papal Palace. What a sight it was, like an imposing castle from a fairy tale with towers, gorgeous doors, gothic windows, and formidable walls. The palace featured narrow vertical openings the length of the walls for archers to defend the church from an invading horde.

We toured the inside courtyard, the sparsely furnished rooms, and the basement treasury. Each pope left his mark by building more additions to the complex, and after the schism was over, the popes returned to Rome. After the popes vacated, the palace was used for different things including a prison and barracks to house soldiers. Towers and other additions to the palace were torn down, and the stones used to build other projects in the area. In the 20th century, renovations were done to restore the palace back to its former glory. They've done an impressive, beautiful job!

For the most part, the museums here are all labeled in French. Few will have both French and English, and others, like the Papal Palace, will be labeled in French with three or four other languages in laminated handouts.

After our visit with the pope, we marched uphill again, story of our trip so far, to the mountaintop palace gardens and the million dollar panoramic view of the Rhone River. From our vantage point, we could see two more castles, the Tour Philippe-le-Bel and the citadel at Villeneuve-lès-Avignon in the far distance. From our vista, we also had a great vantage point to survey the Avignon bridge, the one made famous by the children's song.

Our rule of thumb is we never take the same way home if it can't be helped, you discover more this way. From the top of this hill, we descended down a path, across the top of the city walls, to a spiral staircase in the tower of the old bridge. Leaving out the ground floor of the tower, through the gift shop, we bought a ticket, and traveled through history to the center of the fast moving Rhone river.

Construction started on the Pont Saint-Bénézet in 1171. Half the bridge was destroyed by a flood in 1669, so we stopped where the bridge stopped. It's a beautiful solid old bridge with a small chapel halfway across where St. Bénézet is interred. It would be in your best interest to stop to pray you don't get blown off the bridge and into the swift current. The wind here is very strong.

On the way back down the cobblestone lined bridge, we ducked down onto the observation piers to enjoy a respite from the wind and a view of the fairy tale town and rushing river. From the pier, you can view the imposing towers of the Papal Palace and the fortified city walls, very romantic!

Bathroom Report: The Papal Palace in Avignon had the best restrooms in France so far, but at the Bridge at Avignon was the story which started the famous "Bathroom Reports".

After sightseeing for hours, we both needed to visit the little boy and girl's room, so we followed the international signage for water closet. The arrows for the WC pointed to a courtyard outside the gift shop, and down a flight of three steps. Lis and I walked shoulder to shoulder expecting to be split up once we found Le Femme/Le Homme separate rooms. When we reached the bottom of the three steps, we realized we were IN the one giant mixed gender bathroom. There were men and woman just milling about.

The blended bathroom had two rows of five cubicles down the middle of this room and sinks on the outside walls. The stall walls went all the way down to the floor and well over six feet high. There was no indication one side was men and other for ladies, so when in Rome, go with the flow. It was funny when Lis came out of her cubicle, all guys exited out of her side, and when I came out of mine, there were ladies washing their hands on my side, and no one blinked an eye. This was just another day in a blended bathroom . . . c'est la vie.

After our enriching cultural experience at the mixed bathrooms, Lis and I made our way back through town to McDonald's and ordered using a computer screen. No need to speak French, we just chose our language preference, punched our hamburger of choice, and waited. Our receipt came with a bathroom code on the bottom, but we were good. The computer screens made it easier than trying to talk to someone who may or may not know English. Our McDonald's sandwiches tasted like they do in the U.S. This building had second floor dining, or should I say first floor, because here the first floor is the zero floor, and the second is the first, got it?

I wish they spoke more English at the train stations. Many Europeans speak English as a second language, even the Irish. Usually the person at the information booth speaks a little English, which helps, but all the announcements are done in French; except one time in Nimes, I heard French and Mandarin, I'm like, "Chinese, what the hell?"

On our way home from Avignon, I inquired at the information desk as to which gate we needed for Arles. "C," he said. We made our way to "C", and after about five minutes, there was a long announcement in French during which everyone at our gate disappeared like rats on a sinking ship, uh-oh. So, after one of my brilliant deductions for the obvious, I realized something with our train must have changed. I hurried inside the station to ask a friendly rail worker which gate the train to Arles was at, and with a panicked expression he motioned with his hands to the other side of the tracks. Good thing I asked, the train had just arrived. These trains don't wait around for anyone, even the queen. Good thing we caught this train, the next one was two hours later!

Oasis of Civilization in the Lobby of the Best Western
Sunday, May 15

Most everything is closed Dimanche, it is WINDY, I'm not feeling well, and Lis is starting to have a relapse. She felt normal for two days, but her cough is back. She's rested, and I've emptied the pharmacies for her, but this thing just won't go away. We'll need to see a doctor soon, where do we start?

We waited around the corner of our B&B to catch the bus to the Tourist Information (TI) office. However, we found out public transport doesn't run on Sunday, so we walked uphill to the TI. The TI was open, so we booked a tour of the Camargue for tomorrow. The Camargue is a national park on the Rhone delta, famous for its wild horses, bulls, and flamingos. We heard from some locals the flamingos were extra pink this year.

Bathroom Report: Had a few more bathroom sightings to report on. The TI didn't have a potty, but there was a public one across the street. It was filthy with no lighting and completely dark. You needed to prop the door open for a little light with someone standing guard. There was another freestanding WC across the street on the sidewalk. It was a pay toilette but out of order, so it's back to the dirty one, yeah!

Not desiring to return to our dingy, depressing B&B, we wound up at a Best Western right next to the TI. The "lobby" at our B&B is a like a crowded, dark, garage tool room. We walked into the hotel like we owned the place as to not attract unwanted attention; it had a beautiful, expansive, well-lit lobby. Lis and I ducked into a corner nook and enjoyed their soft leather couches, wonderful clean toilette, €1 electric massage chair, and TV. Lis is still recovering from her cold, and after falling into a deep sleep, she snorted and woke herself up a couple times. The time away from our dismissive host and cold, damp dungeon was peaceful, bright and refreshing. Thank you, Best Western, we love you!

Hankering for lunch, it's off to Subway for a "sammich". There was a group of nine high-school-aged German boys ordering right next to us. When Lisa asked for "lettuce" on her sub, one of the boys covered his mouth and giggled. I know the boy wasn't being disrespectful, his giggle was too innocent. The German boys called the lettuce topping "salad" when they ordered. It's interesting they spoke to the French workers in English. It's a good thing I paid attention in English class.

After lunch, we headed back to our room to relax. Lis did a few loads of laundry to get ready for the big Paris run Wednesday, can't wait. We were worried if the weather was so bad in Arles, which is in the south of France, what would Paris be like way up north? We checked the weather on the computer, and it wasn't looking promising. :(I guess if you were from the northern U.S., this weather wouldn't seem too bad, but if you're from Florida or anywhere warm, this weather might not agree with you.

"Wild" Flamingos, Horses, and the Famous Bulls of the Camargue,
a Delta South of Arles, France
Monday, May 16

We walked to Best Western two hours before the scheduled tour of the Camargue. We needed to escape the dreariness of our dungeon captivity and relax in civilization before the tour started. We met our tour guide, Josette, a native Carmargian who speaks the Provincial dialect of the area. It's a French and Italian mix.

Our new friends on the tour consisted of a Canadian mom and daughter team, a female Chinese student, and her Thai boyfriend. (Both are students in Arles.) Everyone got along nicely, and nobody brought up American politics, hooray. It's so nice to talk English with the Canadians. I swear Brits and Canadians are like family when you meet them in a non-English speaking country on holiday.

The park is only fifteen minutes outside of town, down a few dirt roads and a couple paved. We pulled over to view four wild mares with a young colt, took some pictures, and moved on. Pulled over again, and the horses came right over. For big horses, they were gentle, friendly, and curious. This big male rooted through the Chinese girl's purse, and it looked like he was after her iPad. Once you go Mac you ain't never going back!

Josette pulled over for a herd of bulls, but these wild bulls are not friendly; they killed a tourist three years ago when the genius jumped the fence to get a better photo. I bet he was a finalist for the Darwin Awards that year?

Later we pulled up to a huge herd of about thirty black bulls all wearing bells. When we pulled over, the bulls were walking in unison, and the bells rang like a song; yes, it was a "moment" with music and farm animals.

After about an hour and a half, we came to a coastal town of the Camargue, Les Saintes-Maries de la Mer, surprisingly nice like Cape May, New Jersey, but it's a gypsy pilgrimage site. Gypsies make pilgrimages to a local church basement with a statue of Saint Sarah or the Black Madonna. In this crypt, there are so many candles burning, the room was hot as an oven.

Josette didn't inform us of restaurants or potties, so there's no Bathroom Report this day. Bathrooms are hard to find, especially when most cafes are closed in the afternoon. Nobody needs a bathroom in the afternoon anyway, I guess. Miraculously, I did find decent paella (rice and mixed seafood) at one of the few open cafes. It filled the ole gullet and kept us alive.

Outside of Les Saintes-Maries, the landscape was flat and a bit desolate. The area was sandy, dusty and lacking in lushness. It reminds me of Florida. At home, we drive the country all the time, so we were getting a little bored. On the last leg of the journey, we came upon a huge flock of greater flamingos wading in a shallow lake; thousands in the distance, it was quite a sight. They weren't as pink as ones you see in tourist pamphlets, the bodies were white and wings pink. I've read flamingos are just starting to make a comeback in Florida after a long absence.

Last but not least, Josette pulled over and pointed out an African fly catcher. He was multicolored with orange wings, grey crested head with a yellow strip down the middle, and most striking, an iridescent blue ring around his eyes that continues onto his beak. He's the prettiest bird I've ever seen in the wild! The Camargue has many of the same big wading birds we have in Florida.

Overall, we enjoyed seeing the mammals on our Camargue tour, but the landscape was pretty rugged, dry, and scruffy, similar to where we live in Florida. The ride was bumpy sometimes and the dust would kick up in our faces. We drove with the top down on the Jeep, and although it was fun to peek our heads out of the top for nicer views, the wind did beat us up.

Van Gogh Museum and Packing to Leave Tomorrow for Paris
Tuesday, May 17

Lis had a relapse with her cold, so she slept in and took it easy. While packing for the big move tomorrow to Paris, the sun popped out, and we needed a little light therapy, so it's outside we go.

We've heard in town about the famous Van Gogh exhibition currently in Arles. Time for one last excursion. We headed out our cold, dank hovel, down to the Rhone River, and followed it downstream to Rue Du Docteur Fanton. We followed this less touristy road till we reached the Van Gogh museum.

Two museums, one from Ontario, Canada and the big one from Amsterdam, lent out thirty-two original Vincent Van Gogh's for an exhibition tour. We had a stroke of luck because Arles was one of the stops, and the timing was perfect. The building was a modern design and well air-conditioned just like you'd expect for a posh Van Gogh exhibit. The exhibit brimmed with culture; I just couldn't find the wine and cheese room anywhere? The clientele were good-mannered and respectable and were allowed to get surprisingly close to these originals. We meandered for about an hour; security required everyone to secure our cameras and backpacks in lockers while we toured least we knock anything over.

Van Gogh resided in Arles near the end of his life and completed about 200 paintings, 100 drawings and watercolors of this town, including the famous bright yellow cafe scene. Most of his paintings from Arles had bright colors.

I finally found a good street food vendor right next to the amphitheater. We had no way to cook in our room apart from boiling water, and I was dying for pasta. The food stand carried homemade baked lasagna, which I learned they don't pronounce the same way we do. Lis and I relaxed on a sidewalk bench to eat and people watch.

After our "linner" (late lunch early dinner) we treated ourselves to Provence's own flavors of lavender and violet (they say "wee-o-let") ice cream, and they were surprisingly yummy!!! The wee-o-let ice cream tasted just like the flower. I preferred the lavender and Lis, the wee-o-let!

Back to the dungeon for our final prep and pack for tomorrow's early get up, prison release, and one-mile-walk with all our gear to the Arles regional railroad station for Nimes, for the TGV high speed train to Paris. Night, night. Bon nuit!

Vincent Van Gogh painted this cafe in one of his famous paintings.
Arles, France

The Roman Amphitheater
Arles, France

View of Arles from the top of the Roman Amphitheater

Pedestrian street with the Roman Amphitheater in the distance
Arles, France

The Papal Palace
Avignon, France

*From the Papal Palace gardens we had a view down to the city walls, tower,
Avignon Bridge, and Rhone River*

*View towards the Papal Palace and city walls from the
Avignon Bridge*

Chapter 7

Paris, Here We Come!

Paris is a place in which we can forget ourselves, reinvent, expunge the dead weight of our past. - **Michael Simkins, actor/author**

Local Train from Arles to Nimes, for the TGV Train to Paris
Wednesday, May 18

Last night when we bumped into Pierre, he said he and Nicole would see us off tomorrow morning when we leave for Paris. Needless to say, those two were nowhere to be found when we left the dungeon, not even a sound. Despite the bone chilling, damp cold front and our less than hospitable hosts, Arles was picturesque, historic, and a nice place to visit.

Travel day, so we rose up early, shoved a patisserie bought pastry and coffee down our pie holes, then hiked it to the train station early in the morning. We didn't take the free tourist bus, because we didn't know what direction the bus would take around the circuit once we got on. If it drove counter clockwise, we'd miss the train, so we walked; plus a rare appearance of the sun, and we really needed the heat.

Slugging our way through town, we arrived at the train station; Lis asked the tall railroad station employee for help. He smiled and escorted her to the right machine and pointed to the tiny British flag in the lower right hand corner of the screen. You press the flag for English, and you're good to go.

At around 6' 3", he was the tallest Frenchman we've seen so far. Overall, most people are not very big. This ticket process is a little confusing, so hold on: We paid for the tickets online, then had to print the paper tickets from a stand alone machine at the train station. Now before you get on the train you MUST validate the freshly printed ticket with a different yellow validating machine, or it's a big fine for you.

Lis validated our ticket on the first local train to Nimes, but the big train to Paris she forgot. Thank God the conductor didn't check for ticket validations, or we'd receive a nice €51 fine each for not validating the stupid thing. We've heard that they have no mercy for new tourists.

It was a great idea to be able to reserve specific seats on the train, however, we had no idea how hard it would be to find them!

Each double decker car on the train is either first or second class. We needed to locate the right class car, then the right number (1,2,3), and then our seat, all before the train left the station lickety-split. Some stations have illuminated diagrams on the platform of incoming car order, class, and seating, this one did not.

We found and hopped on the right class car, but realized we were trapped on car number #1, and we needed #3, no problem, right? Stuck in the wrong car, we needed to make our way through two cars of oblivious locals with our elephantine luggage to get to car 3. I had tried to put my luggage in at ground level, but the conductor shook his head, "No, bad people," so it's up the steps with big heavy luggage.

Remember, the French are extremely patient when others stand in their way, but seemingly totally oblivious when they are blocking someone else. They will just stand in your way making small talk with a fellow passenger totally unconcerned to the line of people they're holding up. Sometimes I just wanted to scream.

The regional train from Arles to Nimes took 25 minutes, then a transfer to the Paris/Lyon TGV line for the remaining 2 3/4 hours. Sometimes our TGV high speed rail reached 300 km/hr at times, and again, smooth as silk.

The train rode through the rugged countryside of Provence with fields of blue and yellow flowers, red poppies, white cows, and historical stone homes with terra cotta roofs. Eventually the air conditioning slowly made a difference, and the cabin became comfortable. The TGV has a special snack bar lounge where passengers can stretch their legs and buy snacks and drinks. It's a strange feeling standing in a train when it's traveling 300 km/hr. There's no movies to watch, most people read. As we neared Paris, the landscape became flatter, and we gradually pulled into the city. We made it, we can feel the city vibe. Yeah, we're in Paris!

Our train pulled in at the Paris Gare de Lyon train station. It was enormous, and as we strolled through it, we spotted four French soldiers with rifles guarding a seating area in the station. Apparently this is not normal, and even the locals were confused as to why this was happening? Officials wouldn't let anyone sit in a certain area or walk through it. There seemed to be a lot of confusion.

The funny thing about the subways here is sometimes they have escalators, sometimes they don't. Sometimes down, but not up, sometimes up, but not down, rarely both, sometimes neither, so everybody has to haul their luggage up and down flights of steps. This is why we take lots of naps!

Since Lis is sick, I'm "in charge" of the two big bags, and she has the tickets, small backpack, and shoulder bag with sling we use for travel. I have the giant backpack and large heavy suitcase on wheels, I'm the donkey in Paris, "La hee-haw!"

We're in the Paris Metro, and everyone warned us about pickpockets targeting tourists. Nervous, Lis and I have to separate so she can buy Metro tickets, and a couple scurvy CHUD'S (Cannibalistic Humanoid Underground Dwellers) are hovering around her at the ticket machine, and one guy is leaning and looking while she's putting her info into the machine. Seeing this suspicious CHUD, I dropped the heavy luggage and charged the Cretan like a raging bull, giving the guy the evil eye barking, "Sortez-vous, sortez-vous!" (you get out), and he scurried off.

After our invigorating ticket purchase experience, we descended into the famous Paris "Metro". In order to enter, you must first insert your ticket into the turnstile machine. The ticket is sucked away and pops out three feet in front of you. You must charge through a narrow stainless steel chute, grabbing your validated ticket while escaping before the two cattle doors close on you. It's a similar concept to the guillotine, except it doesn't kill you.

I'm a big fella wearing an enormous backpack and towing a substantial sized heavy luggage container on wheels behind me. After grabbing my validated ticket, I barely got my body through when the cattle doors clamped on and captured my pull behind luggage. Embarrassed and in a panic, I pulled with all my strength, and the metallic jaws would not let go. Thinking quickly on her feet, Lis inserted her ticket into the machine, and in an instant, the evil cyborg released its defenseless prey, and as I yanked the luggage through, Lis followed right behind. Touché Lis, ce bon, I hope nobody saw that!

From Gare de Lyon, it takes two trains to make it to our apartment in the Latin Quarter of the city. We first rode Metro line 1 from the Grande Gare de Lyon station in the direction of Esplanade de La Defense to the Palais Royal Musee du Louvre stop.

At this hub station, we were so close to the Louvre we could almost taste it. From the Louvre, we hopped on Metro line 7 in the direction of Villejuif for our final stop, Censier Daubenton. This last train would takes us to our apartment on Rue Monge ("Rue" is "Street"). The entire Metro experience took about twenty-five minutes.

On our last leg and on our last train, while the doors were still open, an older Muslim man leaned into our car and got in Lisa's face, desperately yelling, "Villejuif, villejuif, villejuif!" Lis was petrified and shook her head as if to say, "I'm terrified and don't know what you're saying," when the "attacker" eyeballed another passenger right behind her, he casually nodded in the affirmative that yes, this train is going in the direction of Villejuif. The "attack" was averted, the muslim man casually sat down by the window, and we were back on our way. It was quite the introduction to the Paris Metro. Next time we have to carry luggage, we'll take a taxi.

We arrived at our Metro stop, Censier Daubenton, up and out into civilization, right onto Rue Monge. When I first heard of Rue Monge, I thought it had to do with food, because "mange" means "to eat" in French. It turns out Gaspard Monge was a famous French mathematician. His name is on the Eiffel Tower.

We gradually got our bearing and walked about three blocks to 95 Rue Monge, Paris. Thankfully it didn't rain like our arrival day in Arles, although it was chilly. Waiting in the lobby of our apartment building for about five minutes, we were met by Aamir, a young Moroccan representative from Airbnb. He showed us around the place and had us sign the lease. Aamir was a courteous, professional young man with excellent English skills.

We love, love, love our little studio apartment in Paris. It's clean, modern, with ample natural lighting from a large window door that led to our petit balcony. This apartment was a far cry from our dungeon nightmare in Arles, like night and day. Our room also overlooked a quiet back street with vintage Parisian buildings across the way.

The buildings across the street are just what I pictured a Paris apartment would look like. They were framed by petit balconies wrapped with black iron, window boxes with flowers, tall narrow windows with beige shutters, and clusters of little chimney pipes popping out of the roof.

The apartment has a mini kitchen inside a built-in cabinet with a coffee maker, water boiler, small fridge, two built-in radiant hot plates, toaster, sink, dishwasher, and cabinets with uncooked food and spices left behind from previous renters.

The apartment was equipped with everything we would need to live, such as silverware, plates, bowls, pots, pans, and drinking glasses. We were not supplied with abundant kitchenware, so we would need to run the little dishwasher everyday.

The apartment came with a king bed, compact table with two chairs, and a modern bathroom with heated towel racks. For clothes, it had a washing machine, folding drying rack, and a closet with sufficient hangers, which makes us both almost giddy! For the same price as a week in a "fancy Nancy" hotel in Paris, we were able to rent this little big apartment for an entire month. With a month's stay we will have plenty of time to savor the Paris ambiance and not having to cram everything in a few days and getting rundown.

Needing to stock up the refrigerator for a month, I headed down to street level to find a grocery store. Exiting our lobby door, turned left, and after taking two steps and before I could exhale my first breath of fresh air, I almost tripped over the ramp into a great little grocery store. This is what I call convenient and cute.

The facade of the Franprix grocery store was end-to-end windows, which allowed what little sunlight there was to brighten up the store. Staring out at you from the inside on the main stage was a refrigerator-sized rotisserie chicken machine with a mountain of cut potatoes underneath the spinning birds. The fat from the rotating chicken would drip and cook the potatoes to a chicken-flavored yumminess.

The grocery store was small, about 30' x 30', clean, well-organized, with fresh produce, and a decent selection of everything we would need in the way of food. You were limited in selection, but everything seemed to be of good quality. Beef wasn't in abundance other than a small selection of really good preformed hamburger and a small seafood selection.

Franprix sold bottled wines and individual cans of beer. The only beer I recognized was Heineken. I sampled one of every beer they carried, about ten, and liked all but one. It tasted like silver polish and was the most expensive. Prices were reasonable overall, I'd say more reasonable than my grocery store in Florida.

Franprix had enough registers to have six cashiers working, but the most I saw at any one time was four. You learned fast the locals at this store like to form a line in the wine and candy aisle and wait their turn. When the first person in line spots an open register, he needs to pay attention and watch. When a seated cashier was good and ready to take another customer, they will look at you, nod their head, wave, or call you over; either way you waited. If you just jump to an open register without being acknowledged, you might get the naughty "look" from the cashier. The cashiers seem to prefer credit cards. One rolled her eyes when I paid with euros. Don't pay with coins, you may not make it out alive.

I carried home all the necessities for the foundation of a month's stay: coffee, cream, butter, milk, cereal (Petals), water, wine, sugar, frozen vegetables, raviolis, rice, preformed hamburgers, and of course one of those delicious rotisserie chicken/potato platters. We stocked the mini-fridge and enjoyed our first lunch in Paris.

The long saga of being sick on this trip came to a head, and we decided to find a doctor for Lis. Her coughing kept her up for the last time, and it's stealing a lot of precious time and energy from our adventure. We visited our local pharmacy and asked where we could find a doctor who could write us a prescription? The pharmacist recommended a medical team just two blocks up the road, and he could squeeze us in if we left right away.

Finding the address, we were a bit confused. The building was very discrete, it didn't resemble a doctor's office we're used to, more like apartments. We buzzed ourselves in, traversed a poorly lit narrow spiral staircase with no hints of a doctor's office, signage, or even a door window or nameplate. "Lis, try the door over there." She opened the door, and an older female patient of the doctor started speaking to us in French. We just smiled and nodded till the doc came in and rescued us.

We were the only patients in the waiting room, and after about five minutes, the doc, whose English was limited, waved us into the office. We pre-translated Lis's symptoms with Google Translate and printed them on an index-sized card, so the doc, who had no help, no nurse, no secretary or translator, checked Lis in, created a file, examined her, printed out a prescription, and collected the cash. Twenty three euros and out the door all under a half hour, bada bing. Back home Lis would have needed x-rays, blood work, cultures, and EKG test all for the low, low cost of $25,000.

The Franprix grocery stores in Paris don't stock aspirin, Robitussin, or Pepto Bismol, etc. You have to find a pharmacy, they're everywhere underneath the flashing green cross. I'm starting to figure out that some of the pharmacists here try to encourage the homeopathic or natural medicines first. One pharmacy representative tried to sell me sinus spray where the active ingredient was capsicum. It's the ingredient in pepper spray that could drop a charging moose. I made a capsicum nose spray mistake back home. It would be considered torture under the Geneva Convention if used on a prisoner. You have to hold your ground here at the pharmacies and read what they are trying to push, and hold out for the good old-fashioned chemical stuff grandma used to make.

Rue Monge street sign
Paris, France

The Franprix grocery store, steps from our apartment in Paris

Chapter 8

Notre Dame

Lisa Rests While Mike Gets Lost Looking for Notre Dame

Friday, May 20

Paris is on the same latitude as the border between Minnesota and Canada, but with the southerly breeze it seems to drag down moisture to make living nice and nasty. We Floridians start to put on sweaters at around 75 degrees. A 57 degree high where I'm from is the apocalypse.

We noticed our Petals cereal box was written in both French and Arabic, and not a hint of English. There's very little English labeling in our petit grocery store.

Lis stayed home and rested to better recover and do a little laundry. The sun was out and shining, so I hit the pavement. Guess who had more fun on our first day in Paris? On a good note,

Lis is finally feeling improved and coughing less. The prescriptions are kicking in.

Late morning I ventured out and meandered around with several failed attempts to make it down to the Seine River. I'm not acclimated to where I am in reference to landmarks and roads in Paris yet, even though I had a general map. It may take me getting lost to get my bearings, so here I go. What makes this city confusing to me is every road is on every angle but a right angle. The city map is like a thousand slices of pie just crammed together. And the few straight roads change names every other block.

I can't waste this beautiful day, so on my third attempt, I finally got my bearings and made it down to the Seine. The river is about forty feet wide where I'm at, brisk flow, green, not pretty green, more like New Jersey ocean green-grey yuck color, but it didn't stink at all. Don't get me wrong, she was majestic with fortified walls to control floods and wide walkways for romantic strolls amongst the historic sites. The style and function was magnificent.

I knew upstream was where the action was, so I huffed it along the cobblestone walkway. As I continued northwest, I came upon the tip of the Île Saint-Louis. It's the small island in the middle of the Seine southeast of the big island of Île de la Cité, where the whole city started.

Well, the Île Saint-Louis is a small island, and a hundred more steps along the river and there she is, the Grand Old Lady, Notre Dame, in the distance like a queen on her throne and definitely walkable. With adrenaline pumping, I pressed on. The closer I get the more enormous and grander she appears. The detail and design are just awe inspiring. Now I see what everybody is talking about, and why this is such a worldwide attraction.

I crossed over a bridge onto the Île Saint-Louis and continued towards Notre Dame and I realized, oh crap, Notre Dame is on a different island, but luckily there was another bridge connecting the two. Up a flight of steps, cross one of those fashionable Parisian bridges, and I'm behind Our Lady. It is spectacular, I can almost hear angels humming. I pinched myself, and this is just the backside. The intricate carvings, the beautiful statues, numerous stained glass windows, and sheer size are breathtaking.

I love architecture, so this is the Super Bowl for me. I can't believe I'm here with thousands of people from all over the world experiencing this masterpiece in 2016. A long line formed to go inside, but I'll wait for tomorrow so I can go with Lis.

Knowing the bread crumbs I left behind would soon be eaten by the birds, I made my way back to the apartment on foot. I wasted 3/4 of my daily energy today getting lost, but I did accidentally discover Rue Mouffetard, a trendy pedestrian road with tons of cafes, bakeries, and cheese shops which we will have to visit later.

Now we know Notre Dame is within walking distance from the apartment, and tomorrow is calling for sun, our adventure is set in stone. Notre Dame, then on to explore the outside of the Louvre, which are just 4 city blocks from each other.

Lisa's Favorite Day So Far: Notre Dame, the Outside of the Louvre, and Our First Bus Ride in Paris
Saturday, May 21

Adrenalized and all geared up by 10:30 am, and it's out the door. Lis is feeling better and wants to hit it hard today. I know the route, and we're on our way with confidence. After a ten-minute walk, we're down at the Seine. You have a choice to walk at water level or street level about twelve feet above; today we chose the water. We continued another two blocks along the river, and we both see her, Notre Dame. Lis is clicking away with her camera the closer we get.

Many of the walking paths in Paris are paved with cobblestone, and along the river there are areas without mortar between the joints. They are a major ankle twisting hazard. You really have to pay attention and watch your step, especially along the Seine.

We cross the Pont St. Louis to Île de la Cité, the big island, to the backyard of Notre Dame, and Lis is going berserk with her camera. Good thing we brought extra memory cards and an external hard drive. Click, click, click, click, the camera's starting to smoke already.

Walking and admiring, we made our way to the front of the church and decide to get in line to go inside. No ticket necessary, Notre Dame is gratuit, merci beaucoup! As the line moves closer to the entrance, we realize mass is going on, the nerve, on a Saturday and in French? The whole thing was surreal, having thousands of tourists snapping pictures at and around you during church service. The priest back home would never tolerate this, never! Some uncouth barbarian tourists were not so respectful during the service and were unceremoniously hushed by paid professional French hushers.

While looking for a way to the roof, we accidentally stood in a line and paid extra to see the church treasury. With the crowds and confusion, we mistook the lines for elevators to the roof, and as most of you know the church doesn't like to give money back. So we made the best of it and checked out the treasury. It contained various implements of gold and silver, paintings, artifacts and documents. We also came face to face with the original statue of martyr St. Denis, holding his own head. I bet that will hurt in the morning. We'll try to do the roof another day when we know what the heck we're doing. We're still wandering around in "Traveler's Fog".

Notre Dame's stained glass windows are impressive, intricate, and abounding in color. She's not the biggest, but Our Lady is the most beautiful cathedral we have seen so far. No wonder it's so popular to visit. Construction began in 1160 and finished in 1345. She is grand, gorgeous, and exquisitely detailed.

The service was done in French, and it was quite moving to hear the congregation singing. After mass was over and while the parishioners exited outside, the organist shifted into a dark, powerful, soul-shaking, Black Sabbath mode. You know the Black Sabbath before Randy Rhodes Black Sabbath. It was so creepy and scary, I swore zombies were going to pop out from under the church floor and start all their zombie nonsense.

Making our way to the exit, we were engulfed in a sea of parishioners heading for Sunday brunch. Good thing we prearranged an emergency meeting point outside, because we became separated. Our meeting place for getting lost was under the Charlemagne statue, so Lis and I met there after a short wait.

The French aren't much into eye contact, they know you're there but have this one mile stare. If you're in their way, they won't say anything, they'll just wait. It's amazing to watch, somewhat too polite. If you say, "Pardon" or "Excusez moi" to them they appear startled, much like a baby deer, and they'll say, "J'desolee" (I'm sorry), smile, and graciously step out of your way.

Most of the French people we interacted with were good-natured, once you break through the privacy bubble they walk around in. Many were like M&M's, hard thin shells on the outside, but sweet in the middle. This cultural difference here will come as a shock to Americans, Canadians, and the Mediterranean folks who are much more outgoing.

With more sunlight and energy, we were on the prowl for more adventure. On one of our maps was the highlighted area of the Square du Vert-Galant and Pont Neuf Bridge at the end of the Île de la Cité, so it's onward ho. It's lunch time, and we're starving. We first stopped to eat in front of the famous St. Michel Monument in the St. Germain section. This spot is a well-known meeting place for locals, and many demonstrations assemble here. We refueled, people watched, and it's off to the end of the island to whatever else we discover.

While strolling up the Left Bank, we came upon Place du Pont Neuf, a famous landmark where couples attach locks to the fence and throw the key in the river to show their undying love for one another. I can't understand how the fence is still standing, it must have a million locks on the darn thing. Many of the locks are engraved or painted with names and dates, the less serious ones are in pencil. This tradition started on Pont des Arts, a pedestrian bridge one block away. When officials became alarmed at the amount of weight these thousands of locks added to the structure, they plexiglassed the area where the locks would go, so the lovers moved here to Place du Pont Neuf near the Henri IV statue.

Taking in all the beautiful sites, I said to Lis, "What's that building over there?"

"The Louvre."

"Where's the pyramid?"

"We must be looking at the backside of the building."

Adrenalin pumping through our veins, we made a beeline for the museum. Along the way while crossing over Pont Neuf, one of those iconic bridges, we beheld for the first time in the distance the Eiffel Tower. We're having tourist overload! We just stared, speechless, taking it all in, it was like a dream. With an accordion player performing behind us on the bridge, it was another awesome moment.

Snapping out of our dreamworld, we entered into the back courtyard of the Louvre. A lone cello played in one of the entrance tunnels. The music echoed off the stone walls. We stood there in a semi-dream state and drank it all in. This was another one of those "magical moments". Two just 15 minutes apart.

The Louvre is "gihunormous", detailed, and grand, and other words not invented yet, and we were in the "boring" part. When we walked through the tunnels to the main courtyard, we were met with all grandeur Louis XIV intended. I can't believe all this was one guy's house at one time?

I sat and people watched and admired the incredible architecture, while Lis clicked away a couple million pictures. I don't have to use words like spectacular, awe-inspiring, grand, magnificent or opulent back home, but I need them here, a lot. The designers of these structures all over Paris made sure your jaw would hit the ground when you encountered their work, and it did.

On the way to the Louvre, we walked past a stop for bus 69. Travel guru Rick Steves suggested using this bus to hit many of the popular tourist destinations. When we finished admiring the outside of the Louvre, we walked back to the bus stop and waited for number 69. After a couple minutes, it pulled up, and we jumped on for the ride. Some bus stops have multiple routes, so make sure you hop on the right bus.

Bus 69 took us through the Marais; past the Carnavalet, Victor Hugo and Picasso museums, the monument marking the location of the Bastille, the Hôtel de Ville, and Père Lachaise Cemetery where Jim Morrison, Edith Piaf, Chopin, Oscar Wilde, and other cool people are buried. The cemetery is high on our priority list, but it will have to wait till another full sunny day.

The bus was a breeze on the way down, though there were about thirty stops, and it took longer than we expected. At the end of the loop, yes in Paris the bus routes had expirations, they kicked us off. We were just going to ride the loop and see all this circuit has to offer. We had to jump on the other bus 69 across the street heading back. The return ride was way more popular and filled up fast with locals. Since the French don't hold air circulation high on the priority list, the bus became stuffy fast, and forget about air conditioning . . . no!

Man oh man, what a cultural experience bus 69 was. I'd write a song if I had any songwriting talent. Twelve more stops, and I swear there's a throng of 70 people on this bus, and all of them breathing. The bus had teeny tiny windows which can open on top of gigantic static windows that don't. What the hell? Whenever the door opened for more people to get on, I would pray to God for just one breath of fresh air.

Finally bus 69 made it to Hôtel de Ville, and we bolted out early for the air, and from there walked back to Notre Dame.

Exhausted but relieved for the fresh air, we plodded our way downstream along the Seine where we encountered a large group of locals singing on our path home. It was a community folk singing choir down by the river. The singing was really quite nice, and would have stayed for a musical "moment", but Lis and I were totally spent with nothing in the tank. We still had to trudge home up Rue Cuvier and the steeper Rue Lacépède to Rue Monge. It's great riding our bikes down the hills, but back up at the end of the day is brutal. Mission accomplished, great day!

On our way into our apartment lobby, we were greeted by the gentle all white lobby cat we named, "Snowflake". Snowflake sits in a glass booth where a security guard would sit if there was one. She protects the vestibule from all trespassers, terrorists, and anyone with cat treats. We don't know who owns this beautiful girl, but she was a sweetheart. Time to relax after a long day of walking and extreme tourist overload!

Rain Day: Jardin des Plantes and Tea at the Grand Mosque in Paris
Sunday, May 22

Weatherman calling for yuck all day, and he was right, so we hunkered down and rested these old bones from all of yesterday's walking. After hanging out all morning, I was getting a little cabin fever. Seeing a glimmer of sun shining down from the clouds, we hustled outside to enjoy the one lonely ray of sunshine. We walked down six blocks to the nearby public park, Jardin des Plantes, to see what it was all about. This park has a small zoo and natural history museum, but both are closed on Sunday.

We walked down the long lanes lined with evenly spaced manicured trees. The sides of the trees were trimmed straight, so they looked like boxes. Lis beamed when she passed roses growing on trellises in a side area and another section of irises which reminded her of Grandma's garden. The entire park was geometrically designed with flower beds down the center. Because it started to rain, we headed home early, but hopefully we'll return to explore more. The Natural History Museum we discovered on the way out displayed an enormous animal tooth taller than Lisa. It looked like a seven-foot tooth from a prehistoric tiger.

After taking in the day's five minutes of sun, it rained, so we made our way next door to the Grand Mosque for cinnamon tea in their garden cafe. We loved the ambiance, and the service was prompt. I asked Khalid, our waiter, if we could go into the Mosque? It's advertised as a working museum, and he smiled and waved us in. The inside of the Mosque was impressive, the layout was elegant with a garden running down the middle, working fountains, and a beautiful emerald green tile courtyard. We felt as though we were in Morocco.

On the inside walls were plaques dedicated to the fallen muslim soldiers who fought for France in the last 100 years of war. Everyone was welcoming and friendly until we walked toward what looked to be the grand prayer room, and a gnarly old caretaker yelled at us from across the garden, in Arabic no less. We're used to being yelled at in French by now, but this is new. A tall North African fellow, dressed in white from head to toe, relayed to me the caretaker wants me to talk to him. We walked over, and the caretaker pointed to the schedule on the wall which listed the visiting hours of 9:00-14:00 and 16:00-20:00, and guess what time it was? It was 15:40, our luck, could you believe it? He said come back later at 16:00. That was the first time we were yelled at in Arabic, I guess there's a first for everything.

Now it gets really interesting. As we leave the mosque, there are four French Army soldiers fully geared up with body armor, camouflage uniforms, and their odd-looking rifles, posted at the front entrance to the mosque. Everywhere we go the French Army seems to follows us. I feel like Napoleon. Now, there were no soldiers when we entered, but appeared when we exited?

We're seeing soldiers at many of the big tourist sites: the Louvre, Notre Dame, the Invalides, the Grand Mosque, etc. The French government wants them visible so the public feels safe. Most of the time they end up helping tourists with directions, and they just walk around with not much happening.

*View towards Notre Dame along the walkway of the Seine River in Paris, France
Later this area was totally submerged in the flood.*

*Notre Dame and the Seine River before the flood
Paris, France*

*Love locks at the Place du Pont Neuf
Paris, France*

*Our Paris apartment lobby mascot,
"Snowflake"*

From inside the Grand Mosque in the Latin Quarter
Paris, France

Chapter 9

Louvre

Another Rainy Day, Off to the Inside of the Louvre

Monday, May 23

Game plan set, it's off to the inside of the Louvre. The weatherman's calling for rain, so it's a good day to take the underground Metro to the museum and stay indoors. The Metro drops you off right inside a modern mall under the Louvre. Once we made it to our Metro station two blocks away on our street, we avoided the rain the rest of the day.

Travel guides say it's crazy busy in the morning at the Louvre, so we took our time. Having time to kill, I ran out in the morning for a much needed haircut. It's been difficult for me to get a haircut in France. I searched in Antibes and Nice with no luck.

When a shop was open, the hairdressers were usually sitting down and on a break.

Down across from Jardin des Plantes, I found a coiffeur whom we passed every time we walked to the Seine. My beautician, in her early 60's, was a bit dismissive, and after sneering at my Google translation for my styling request, she sat me down and began to cut my hair. She did a nice job, but never uttered a word, smiled, or even looked at me. Even as I paid, her head was turned. I said, "Merci beaucoup," and left. We would pass by this coiffeur quite a few times a week, and she was never with another customer again, I wonder why?

When I returned with my snazzy new French haircut, we headed off to the Metro in the pouring rain. With streams of water cascading down the outdoor entrance escalators, we descended into the Metro. Six always interesting stops, and we arrived at the mall at 11:30, and proceeded to stand in line for what seemed three lifetimes. This line was a football field long and moving slow.

The ticket counter had 3 ladies working at the front, and they all seemed to wait on the same one person or couple at a time. The ticket information pamphlet you need to make educated purchasing decisions was right at the cashier. Moving the display back just ten feet would give the crowds time to decide their options. Yeah, but that would speed up the whole process, and we're in France, ugh.

After we secured our tickets, it's time to stand in another line for security. They're a lot like the TSA, all theater. To date zero terrorists caught. After security, it's into this world famous colossus of a museum and icon of France. The art was amazing; the artifacts from Egypt, Iraq, and Syria were my favorites. We focused most of the day in the Richelieu wing, one of three wings of the Louvre which took about three hours on our feet. The Richelieu wing doesn't display any of the "superstar" exhibits, but we enjoyed them nonetheless.

Digging down deep for energy at the end of the day, we decided to take on part of the Sully wing and were there for another two hours. No, we didn't see the Mona Lisa yet, this place is "gihumungus".

We really wanted to see the 14 foot tall ancient Winged Bulls of Assyria. King Sargon II mounted them, flanking his royal throne room. Though we saw the bulls on the first floor from the upper level of the Richelieu wing, it still took us a couple hours of winding up and down and around the museum to find our way to the exhibit. Traversing the Louvre is a lot like the *Indiana Jones the Temple of Doom* movie. Plenty of basements, mummies, and secret passages to keep you lost.

The museum has an interesting way of labeling each floor, they're marked -2, -1, 0, 1, 2; zero being ground floor. The layout here is pretty confusing, due to each successive king's made changes and additions. It's not just three or four flat floors that go straight across, no, that would make sense. The floors are broken up with dead ends in the middle of your run, so to continue across you have to go up, over, and then down to continue on the original floor. It could be very confusing, sometimes we had to look out a window just to get our bearings.

One of Lisa's favorite places in the Louvre was Napoleon III's apartment. It occupied an elegant section of the palace, like Versailles with all the fancy ceiling paintings, mirrors, candelabras and ornate decorations. It was impressive, it's good to be the Emperor!

Napoleon's dining room could seat 46 of the most beautiful and important of people. His personal apartment overlooked the front of the Louvre where the pyramid stands today. We could see the Eiffel Tower from his grand room in the far distance. Napoleon III never could because it wasn't built yet.

We both appreciated the ancient art. Much of the colors on the glyphs still remain after three thousand years. It was impressive, especially since I have to paint my house every eight years? We can see why the Louvre is considered the greatest art museum in Europe, it's huge! The architecture of the Louvre is just as beautiful as the artwork inside. We'll definitely come back another day to explore what we've missed, next time using the Museum Pass to skip the long line. We still have to find the Mona Lisa, Winged Victory, and Venus De Milo to see what it's all about. We ended up passing through and seeing all the magnificent life-sized sculptures in the Grand Gallery a couple times. We kept getting lost and going in circles, like the Griswalds in *European Vacation*.

On one of the upper floors in the Richelieu wing, we observed ten student painters with their easels, brushes, and canvases in front of exhibited paintings, copying some of the old masters. From what we could observe, they were highly skilled. On each easel were signs saying, "No Pictures" and "Do not disturb the artist." It must be a great honor to be chosen as one of these painters.

The long awaited Bathroom Report: If you stand in line for museum tickets at the underground mall, you will be with about 20,000 other people. If you need the potty while in line, you'll walk around and look for WC or Toilette signs. Don't expect to find a bathroom at the food court, that would be silly. The WTH moment came when I discovered the bathroom is promoted as a "spa" and charged €1,50. The "spa" has a male and female attendant, and a gender appropriate attendant will pull the curtain aside for you to go in . . . oh, now I see what the €1.50 was for. Don't look to get your hair or nails done here, it's just bathrooms.

Oh yeah, to find this WC (Water Closet), the sign at the bottom escalator pointed down, but there was no down or steps to go down, or elevator, just solid floor, it was maddening.

After I returned, Lis went off and found a different bathroom in the mall where they only charged €1. She didn't have a fancy attendant like I did. She said both men and women waited in line together to pay and then to separate bathroom sections. However, to go to the ladies' section, Lis had to pass the men's room, which had no door, and the urinals were right there within sight for everyone to see. Vive la Eek!

The WC's inside the Louvre are free, but not well marked or plentiful. They only have about a million visitors a day. Who needs bathrooms, right? Back in the day, the royals and court would relieve themselves in stairwells and out of the way places when nature called. It must have smelled wonderful?

Time to go home and rest our feet. We walked for about five hours in the Louvre. Thankfully the rain stopped by the time we exited out the Metro. Our apartment is only two blocks from the stop, "Place Monge".

Water Taxi to the Eiffel Tower
Tuesday, May 24

My bucket list for years included a river cruise up the Seine from Normandy to Paris. They are pricey, so we settled for the river taxi "on and off" boat up the Seine. This morning we hit the road and walked to the river, and purchased a two day pass for the "on off" river taxi, called the Batobus. Our taxi was a long, glass-covered barge which held about two hundred people comfortably. It stops at all the big sights along the Seine: the Eiffel Tower, Musée d'Orsay, St. Germain, Notre Dame, Hôtel de Ville, Louvre, Champs-Élysées, Beaugrenelle, and our home stop, Jardin des Plantes.

Our main goal today was the Eiffel Tower, and after sailing the Batobus under twenty ornate bridges, there it was in the near distance, and as we got closer it became larger and larger. "Man, the Eiffel Tower is flippin huge!" It really took my breath away. We piled out of the water taxi and walked up about forty stairs to ground level with the tower, and oh my God, we are actually here and it's humungous. I can't believe this was originally built as a "temporary" structure for the 1889 World's Fair, and it's still here?

This "iron lace" tower is so big and spectacular, pictures can never do it justice as with so many things here. So much work and steel went into making this grand structure, you just stand there in amazement. The people at the first observation level look like ants to us on the ground. We were standing at probably the world's most iconic structure in the world, and I am in awe!

For two hours, we took in the tower from both the Parc du Champ de Mars, a large park area next to the tower, and the Trocadéro Gardens across the river, the most amazing views from both areas.

Here at the tower, as with the Louvre, there is a cadre of African guys selling miniature Eiffel Towers. They can be a little annoying at times, but if you say no they leave you alone and move on. They are just trying to make an honest euro. Today while at the tower, all the African vendors started to run like there was no tomorrow. It appears occasionally the police raid these guys, who I presume need permits.

When we felt hungry, I found a mobile crepe vendor on the Champ de Mars park, so we stood in line for a chicken and cheese crepe. There was a young Spanish lady in front of me, and when it was her turn to order she asked for a cheese and chocolate crepe. The manager, who only handled the money and orders, shook his head and said, "No." You heard right, NO. The perplexed customer paused and looked around to see if he was joking (he wasn't), so she timidly changed her order to something more "acceptable" to the manager. The female employee actually making the crepes rolled her eyes in disgust, smirked, and whispered to the customer, "It sounds good to me," but still couldn't get what she wanted while the Crepe Nazi watched.

While walking back under the Eiffel Tower, Lisa took more pictures. You see, as time goes by, the angle of the sun is different, so if you captured a picture an hour ago and then take another from the same place, the picture will have a completely different look and feel to it due to the angle of the sun.

When I stood by the ticket line for the tower to people watch, an African father walked towards me with his adorable, chubby three-year-old daughter who was walking behind him sobbing. Not a tantrum, but a soul-crushing pain in her little heart. Since my French is limited, I'm going to have to take the liberty to read their expressions and tones. The little girl really wanted something for some reason the father couldn't provide at that moment, her little heart was breaking. Never have I empathized so much with a hurting child as with her that day. She desired something so great, it pained her heart so much, she sobbed and sobbed. The father was so gentle and tender with her little heart. He wasn't frustrated, angry, threatening, dismissive, or cold. He was a hero to me, that sunny day under the Eiffel Tower. This was my most memorable human moment of the whole trip.

After about three hundred pictures between the two of us and twenty-nine offers to buy miniature towers, string tricks, and character drawings from peddlers, it was off toward the Louvre to see the Tuileries Gardens. So it's back on the boat and to the Louvre. The Tuileries offered us a peaceful break from all the automobile traffic. Lis liked the manicured tree lanes, so we rested with the locals at a fancy fountain.

At the end of the Tuileries, you'll find a ferris wheel giving tourists great vistas of the city. There's also an Egyptian obelisk which was dedicated to Louis XVI and Marie Antoinette. They were beheaded along with about two thousand others during the Reign of Terror. The king, Louis-Philippe who came to power temporarily after Napoleon's first exile and before his escape from Elbe, erected the monument in 1836.

The obelisk, from the temple of Luxor in Egypt, was transported in a giant wooden box which was engineered to travel down the Nile, across the Mediterranean Sea and Atlantic Ocean, and up the Seine. It had gold leaf reliefs on the bottom of the column illustrating how it was transported. The two mind-boggling mysteries of this day were: why an Egyptian obelisk for a murdered Bourbon king, and why haven't I seen a bathroom in six hours, for the love of God!

The obelisk sat on a raised concrete circle area on the road between the Champs-Élysées and the Tuileries Garden, called the Place de la Concorde, just a stone's throw from the big ferris wheel. It seems like the entire Right Bank traffic merges onto this ten lane circle, and it's a madhouse.   In order to cross most streets, pedestrians had to wait for the "green walking man" display light up on a pole facing them.   We never witnessed police ticketing pedestrians, let alone us jaywalkers.

Beautifully ornate fountains flanked each end of the circle. We could see the Arc de Triomphe way down in the distance down the Champs-Élysées.   I hope to see that bad boy up close and personal on a sunny day.

We were pre-warned that "every" Parisian smoked . . . a lot. Images of a 1970's bar with L.A. type smog gagging us Americans kept me up at night.   After being here for a while, we realized smoking wasn't much more than the States.   The pace on the street was slower than I expected.   It was comfortable, most didn't seem to be pressured or in a big hurry, highly professional.   We were also warned about dog poop, and yes, there were the occasional watch your step moments, but not more than any other city or suburb I've been to.   So much is blown out of proportion.   I swear, some people get a kick out of peddling fear.

Exhausted from all the walking, we headed back to the apartment via the Batobus, so we sailed down the Seine for a three hour nap before bedtime. This "city living" is going to take a bit of getting used to.

Bike to Champs-Élysées and Found Le Petit Palais
Wednesday, May 25

We rented bikes at the nearest Velib docking station to our apartment for the first time this morning. It was only three blocks up Rue Monge. Once you find the unmanned terminal, press five on the screen for English, push your credit card all the way in the receiving slot, and the rest was just "follow the directions". It's €8 a week, and free for the first thirty minutes, after that €1. You must wait 2 minutes after docking to remove your bike again to keep it free. If you watch your time, and return your bike to any of the hundreds of docking stations all around the city, renting a bike in Paris would only cost you €8 a week.

As we travel the roads and sidewalks of Paris, we have noticed a small number of Parisians like to purposely get in your way when you walk or bike near them. Also some cars (not all) will speed up and turn right in front of bikes who are going straight and cut them off. This happened a couple times to Lis, but not to me. I guess the owners of those cute little cars didn't want a guy my size slamming into the side of their tiny Peugeots or Citrions. The poor little things would be demolished with no chance of survivors.

Down to the Seine, past Notre Dame, over to the Right Bank, we chuckled at the wide-eyed tourists and the pigeon man entertaining the kids with his semi-trained flock of over-fed birds. At the Louvre, we continued on through the Tuileries Gardens, kicking up dust along the way.

We found out later, dust is a major problem at the local museum, and we were told to walk our bikes by an official-looking guy with a red armband. So we dismounted and walked our way to the nearest side street, hopped back on our awesome Velib rentals, and continued on our way.

Driving up the Champs-Élysées was grueling, and after about ten crowded, nerve-racking blocks, we realized nobody else is riding bikes there, oops? We didn't notice any signs forbidding bikes, but with the massive crowds and traffic, we concluded this famous avenue wasn't bike friendly. So we doubled back away from the Arc de Triomphe and returned the bikes to their secure electronic bays. We made sure we heard the beep and saw the green light that confirmed a completed transaction. From there we walked.

While wandering back toward the Place de la Concorde, we stumbled upon Le Petit Palace. This museum, in the 8th arrondissement, was one of many structures built for the 1900 Exposition Universelle. The entrance looks like what you might imagine "Heaven's Gates" must be: tall ornamental golden gate with angels under an arched limestone entranceway. After picking up our jaws from the sidewalk, we went inside (free).

We found ourselves walking around Paris with our eyes bugged out and mouths hanging open all the time. The paintings and sculptures were stunning and from the most well-known names in history. I have to say the building containing the art was just as much a masterpiece as the art in itself, simply gorgeous. We really enjoyed the garden courtyard inside, the ceiling with its dream-like murals, and decorative plaster ornamentation.

Across the street from La Petit Palace was Le Grand Palais, which was also built for the 1900 Exposition Universelle. It had numerous ornate glass and ironwork structures on the roof, which was impressive and can be seen from far away. The Grand Palais, one of 130 museums in Paris, holds temporary art exhibits throughout the year. At this particular time, Le Grand Palais held an exhibit of modern art, so we passed. We like some modern art, but there's so much to see. It wasn't on our "A" list, so we moved on.

Time to head home, Lis suggested we take the Batobus instead of the bikes, and I agreed. But because of where we boarded, it ended up taking us the opposite direction and took us about two hours to get to our home stop, egh. At least we were able to sit and capture more pictures of the Eiffel Tower from the water taxi in dissimilar lighting; same goes for Notre Dame. We returned home totally exhausted again, time to rest up before bed!

Les Invalides, Napoleon's Grave, the Military Museum, and
Luxembourg Gardens. Le Grand Tour!
26/5/2016: You Read it Right,
That's How the Europeans Write Dates

Sun is as rare here in Paris as spontaneous French smiles on
the streets this time of year. We're off to Napoleon's tomb and
Army Museum at the Hôtel des Invalides.

We're really starting to get the hang of the rental bike
system, so we peddled down to the Seine toward the Louvre,
turning left along the river, looking for Rue Invalides, which we
never found. We turned and headed south, and stumbled upon a
portion of Embassy row with all the official-looking buildings and
flags. We passed the embassies of Colombia, Canada, and England.
There were scores of important looking people in suits walking
around with "Diplomatic Immunity".

We finally stumbled on our goal, the School of Military at
the Invalides. It was hard to miss with all the cannons and real
soldiers walking around in full gear. The soldiers seem to be on
high alert here in Paris for some reason.

The Hôtel des Invalides was originally built in 1670 by Louis
XIV to house disabled soldiers and veterans. The Chapel of St.
Louis inside is really two churches; the humble one was for the
soldiers and the other more opulent was for the King. Today the
"King's Chapel" is where the tomb of Napoleon stands. You can see

the gold dome glisten all the way down to the Seine. The rest of the complex houses the Army Museum.

The Army Museum was pretty impressive, but we only had time to visit the 1800's era wing of the museum. We noticed from the authentic military uniforms of the period, the soldiers of the time were so much smaller than today, almost child size. It was a sobering moment realizing many of them were just kids.

A lot of scratch went into Napoleon's final resting place; for a guy who distressed much of Austria, Italy, Spain, Prussia, Egypt, England, France, and half of Russia. The place was grand, almost Vatican-like, with marble floors, relief decorated walls, twelve Greek statues, all under an imposing gold dome. His quartzite marble sarcophagus is centered under the enormous circular dome of Les Invalides. I took my first selfie in my life here; hey, it's Napoleon's grave, I couldn't help it.

Leaving the military museum, we traveled to the nearby iconic Alexander III bridge, which spans the Seine across from the Grand Palais. It presents gold embossed statues of Pegasus standing guard on each of its four corners, and garland-like carvings with men's faces at every knot. Just crossing a bridge in Paris is a culturally enriching lifetime experience. This bridge was built to honor the Franco-Russian alliance in 1892, and Czar Nicholas II himself laid the foundation stone. We crossed over this bridge often.

Driving from our apartment along the Seine is one-way traffic toward Notre Dame. There are ample sidewalks, sometimes twenty feet wide. Heading home, we unfortunately have to peddle against the grain. Sometimes with the multiple bouquinistes (book venders), bus stops, and occasional narrowness, it can become a little congested.

Some roads have designated bus, bike, and taxi lanes, which really come in handy. Lis had a surly old Frenchman swear at her today in beautiful English, while she rode her bike the wrong direction. I told Lis when we leave this country, the Parisian drivers will shoot off fireworks from the Eiffel Tower.

We grabbed another Velib bike and on to Luxembourg Gardens. The twenty-three hectare gardens were a pleasant and peaceful oasis in the middle of the 6th arrondissement. We rested where the children sail the rented miniature boats seen in all the tourist brochures. It must be really delightful here in August when the sun comes out. Today the gardens displayed newly planted flowers. I'm sure later in the summer they will be more magnificent after they fill in. For being the largest city in Europe, it rarely seems crowded, except in line for the Louvre or inside Bus 69.

Bathroom Report: Paris has a few of these freestanding Sanisettes bathrooms. They're light brown oval structures usually on the sidewalk. At no cost you can use one of these private rooms, but you'll have to wait until it cleans itself after every use, so there's normally a line. If you rush in after someones steps out without waiting for the rinse cycle, you'll enjoy a shower at no extra charge. So if patience isn't your thing, try a cafe.

View from the Denon Wing towards the Richelieu Wing of the Louvre
Paris, France

The Batobus water taxi
Seine River, Paris, France

*The Eiffel Tower seen from the Champ de Mars park
Paris, France*

*Champs-Élysées looking toward the Place de la Concorde
Paris, France*

La Petit Palais near the Alexander III Bridge
Paris, France

Elaborate sculptures at the Alexander III Bridge
Paris, France

Napoleon's grave under the gold dome of the Hôtel des Invalides
Paris, France

Toy sailboat and palace at the Luxembourg Gardens
Paris, France

Chapter 10

Père Lachaise Cemetery and the Opera

Père Lachaise Cemetery and the Opera
Friday, May 27

Today's primary goal is the famous Père Lachaise Cemetery, secondary is the L'Opera. This morning Lis and I studied the metro and bus map like Napoleon preparing for a battle, and we figured along with the Metro, bus, and Velib bike rentals we could probably get anywhere in the city.

Before we left our room, we decided it might be easier just to take the Metro from our apartment to the Opera. We'd transfer to another Metro line that takes us straight to the cemetery, that's the plan anyway. Trains are every three minutes, so if you miss one, there's another one right behind it.

We don't love or hate the Metro or the bus, but depending on the weather and length of trip, we chose our poison. If it's nice out, we love the bikes, as long as it's with traffic flow and our location has the Velib docking stations nearby. Sometimes we'd take the bikes one way and a bus on the way home for safety reasons. The Arc de Triomphe and the Champs-Élysées didn't have docking stations nearby, so we took the Metro. Public transportation maps can be pretty intimidating at first, but with time we were making our transportation decisions more confidently and with less stress.

The gods have spoken, out the door, across the street, and up two blocks to Place Monge Metro stop line 7, down the steps, through the cattle doors, no pick pockets, and on the train with the locals toward La Courneuve. When we entered our Place Monge subway, there appeared to be a woman "stuck" in-between the turnstile and the cattle doors. Only having three lanes to choose from, Lis put her ticket in the channel with the trapped woman, and bam, the doors opened and she took off through the horse doors like a thoroughbred on race day on Lisa's dime, without as much as a merci. Either this was a scam, or she put in an expired ticket and really got trapped. Well Lis was out a €1.49 ticket and a cheap life lesson. Now Lis had to use a second ticket to get herself through, the Metro won't honor her boo-boo.

After five stops, we jumped off line 1 and transferred onto line 3 at the Opera hub heading toward Gallieni. We took line 3 all the way to the Gambetta stop. Travel Guru Rick Steves says if you wait and get off at Gambetta and not Père Lachaise, you'll walk downhill and not uphill all the way through the cemetery. Out from the dark underworld of the Metro into the light, we continued on only two blocks, and there it is, Père Lachaise, can't miss it. Good thing we are going downhill, because this cemetery is huge!

Walking through the main gate, we stopped at the map display case to read the posted locations of where all the famous dead people were interred. While we were planning, a nice American couple walked up and handed us their map they purchased at the other entrance. Hmm, this day is starting well.

The old world cemeteries used to put a lot of artistic effort into their headstones, well, those who could afford to did, and many were exquisitely crafted. Many of the graves here were moss-covered since there's scores of shade trees and rain. Even the moss in Paris is artistic!

The first famous person's monument we came to was Oscar Wilde. I'm not too familiar with the guy, but he used to get so many women kissing his monument, the family installed plexiglass around it. They installed the glass, because they had to pay to clean off the lipstick. When we visited, there were about thirty lipstick marks on the plexiglass. Others leaned over top the high glass and kissed the stone itself.

Following the map, we happened on the grave of Edith Piaf, who sang "La Vie en Rose" and "Non, Je Ne Regrette Rien", the latter can be heard in the movie, *Saving Private Ryan*. Edith was raised in a brothel, and at the age of fourteen she joined her father who was a street performing acrobat. Edith traveled all over France and sang on the streets. After being discovered in 1935, she became world famous. Her gravesite was humble and easy to miss, but with fresh flowers on top and planted flowers all around.

Lis and I are getting a little hungry. "Let's have a little lunch here on the bench, nobody will mind, they're all dead." Well, I finished my lunch, but while Lis was still munching on her "sammich" (Jersey slang for sandwich) Ms. Flaming-red-haired-tour-guide-nazi-lady yelled something to her in French. All I understood was 'manger' (to eat) and la blah, la blah, la blah as she pointed to the gate from which we came. She was either saying get out, or didn't you idiots read the rules at the entrance? Either way we agreed, smiled, waved and finished our lunch. If there was a list of rules at the gate, I guarantee it was only in French, and my French stinks. Another day another upset local, c'est la vie!

We had to do it because we're here, so we made a pilgrimage to Jim Morrison's gravesite to see what all the hubbub was about. The surprisingly unassuming gravesite is cordoned off with metal barricades. Pilgrims tie colored strings around the barricade and leave chewed gum and mementos for ole Jimbo. When we arrived, there were two other couples paying homage; the one couple in their thirties who spoke in Spanish appeared as though they may have slept in coffins the previous night. Both dressed all in black, and she wore five-inch tall Herman Munster shoes.

Before we left, Lis wanted to see Pointillist George Seurat's family resting place. Seurat's painting style was most unique. He'd place one dot of paint next to a different dot of paint to get a totally different color when you step back. For instance, a red dot next to a blue dot gives you purple at a distance. Seurat's most famous painting, "A Sunday Afternoon on the Island of La Grande Jatte", was a painting of a park along the Seine just upstream of the Eiffel Tower. Today, this painting is exhibited in the Art Institute of Chicago. When Lis was in college, she visited the museum and came face to face with this masterpiece. The painting was most impressive at seven feet by ten feet.

Enough death and coffin sleepers, it's off to the Metro and on to the famous L'Opera Garnier. This time our stairs to the Metro were in the middle of the street. It's into the pit looking for line 3 again and backtracking, because we passed the Opera getting to the cemetery.

While on our way to the Metro, a street vender greeted us with, "Guten tag." He must have mistaken us for Germans. Perhaps we're starting to get that fashionable European swagger and one mile stare?

Ten lightning quick stops, no, I'm kidding, it was a long fifteen minute ride on a crowded subway. Lots of good people watching today, and some bad people smelling. Lis was stuck sitting next to a young guy who smelled like he hadn't showered or washed his clothes in quite a while. Good thing stinky got off before we did, so Lis could compose herself and get a couple breaths of fresh air before hitting the bricks. Smelly people are

NOT the norm in Paris, but when you do meet one, and they sit next to you, it's a long ride.

The Parisians on a whole are a pretty reserved lot, that is until they argue on the phone. They'll be screaming bloody murder for the whole city to hear; windows would rattle, pets would flee, and no one blinks an eye. We've witnessed this on more than one occasion, like today on the Metro.

Climbing out of the subway to a bustling street in the 9th arrondissement, we turned around and WOW, there she is, L'Opera Garnier, like a queen at her coronation. Sitting there in all her majesty with two golden angel statues guarding Apollo atop her green patina crown.

L'Opera proudly boasted of her famous composer suiters, with busts of Mozart, Beethoven, Rossini, Auber, Meyerbeer, Spontini, and Halévy prominently ensconced halfway up the facade. Each legend between two Corinthian columns. Among the hordes of tourists, we waited for the blinking red man crossing signal to turn green; when he did, we shot across the street and made our way to L'Opera.

Entering in through the back door, we purchased a ticket from an automated machine, and proceeded in. Every museum we go into we get searched, with metal detectors and peek-a-boo bag officials. Some inspectors are really nonchalant and bored stiff, while others are serious and sometimes downright nosey.

The inside of L'Opera was breathtaking, on the edge of over the top, but still stunning. Opulence, luxury, and splendor in the

Beaux art motif, on every wall, every stairway, and even the ceiling. Marble floors and columns reflected light from the scores of mounted candelabras and chandeliers. You can almost imagine the drama among the upperclass of Paris as they'd jostle for choice positions on the grand stairway or lobby before a show. The lobby was purposely designed for the flower of the upper society to see and to be seen.

We couldn't enter the main auditorium due to a soundcheck taking place, but we could peek through a tiny window inside one of the private booths. The stage was unusually deep, seating limited, and the grand chandelier hung below a famous Marc Chagall ceiling painting. It was a good day, it was a wonderful day!

Easy Day Strolling the Streets of Paris
Saturday, May 28

With the prospect of rain in the forecast, we decided a leisurely stroll through the Old City was what the doctored ordered. Just hoist the mainsail and go where the wind takes us today. Sometimes the best things are discovered without schedule or plans.

Our latest nifty travel discovery was Bus #47 which can be picked up right next to the Velib bike rental docking stations on our street. I watched #47 pass right by our apartment a hundred times.

"Hey, I wonder where that could take us?" The map at the bus stop showed the route, and I thought, *"This bus will work out nicely."*

Using one billet each, we hopped on #47 and headed toward the Île de la Cité, the center of the historic area. We got off next to Square René Viviani, a small park across the street from the Seine. After a leisurely walk through this petit oasis of green trees, red rose bushes, and mossy concrete benches was one of the coolest, "mostest", trendiest places in St. Germain for English readers, the former beatnik enclave of Shakespeare and Company bookstore and cafe.

Shakespeare and Company can be found at the corner of Rue de la Bûcherie and Rue Saint Julien le Pauvre. The cafe appears to be newer, and with the views of Notre Dame, writers' inspiration is flowing like the Seine in spring.

The character of this former monastery is amazing, and characters who have passed over these thresholds must be legendary. For aspiring writers, this place is Mecca. Here is where young avant-guard writers have come to catch that creative mojo.

This is not only the coolest independent bookstore in town . . . wait for it . . . wait for it, it also provides free rooms for economically-challenged young writers willing to put a little time helping out in the store. These writers, known as Tumbleweeds, in lieu of rent must also read a book a day and write a short autobiography for the store's archives.

The oldest portion of Shakespeare and Company, which opened in 1951, occupies two of the three store fronts. Two large windows outlined with hunter green trim sport chalkboards for shutters with the founder's inspirational story. The gold background exudes the warm bohemian history from its beatnik past.

Entering into this historic old bookstore, you glide along a mosaic of what appears to be recovered demolition tiles, some whole and ornate, others just shards. This hodgepodge mosaic walkway snakes you through a wonderland of colors, stories, and hand drawn art. Second-hand chandeliers light your way, and rustic handmade shelves, floor to ceiling, display mostly used novels. Some of these books are older than me, and from all over the English-speaking world.

The narrow creaky stairway to the second floor still carries the spirits of many a starving writer and curious tourist. Upstairs is a continuation of the downstairs ambiance with rows of classic old books with sleeping cots, stand up piano, and an antique chair acting as a desk supporting an old-fashioned ribbon typewriter.

After our jaunt through beatnik history, we strolled the people-packed pathways along the Seine. Just around the corner from S&C is my favorite little narrow alleyway named Rue du Chat-qui-Pêche, or "The Road of the Fishing Cat", I just love the name. It's technically a road at only five feet in width. We rested like locals at Place Saint Michel, a major intersection for the legions of adrenaline-pumped tourists. It's fun to just imagine where everyone is coming from.

Cold and Damp Weather at Jardin des Plantes
Sunday, May 29

Our old bodies are so beat up and exasperated from the cold, damp weather and sickness, we decided to head home after the full month in Paris. Our next destination was supposed to be the Loire Valley, but it was so flooded from all the continuous rain, we canceled our B&B there and Normandy. We also secured our flight home with United. England and Germany will have to wait, but any more northern European trips will have to be in August when the sun comes out.

With today's cold and damp weather, we hunkered down in our room till lunch, then decided to bundle up and slog through the rain down to Jardin des Plantes, our neighborhood city park about six blocks away. The park contains a small zoo, but it was just too miserable to enjoy the critters. We just wandered around and acquired a perspective of where things were in this part of the Latin Quarter.

This is the crazy type of weather that's too damp to bundle up because you would sweat, and too cold to layer thin. If a gust of cold wind hits you while you're dressed minimal, it just chills you to the bone. Wear too much, you sweat out of your clothes. Many of the locals seem to go light, so they don't sweat, they just endure the cold. These Parisians must be hardy folks, not many people wearing hats and gloves on the streets.

It's a good thing Lis brought her scarf, she almost didn't pack it. We have to be careful so we don't get sick (again). No sun, cold, and damp, so it's an easy day today. We've lost so much motivation in this weather. We live in Florida, and a cold day there is 70 degrees, not a high of 57.

Miserable Weather So We Rest in Our Apartment
Monday, May 30

Another miserable day, and they're calling for the same tomorrow: cold, damp, and rainy, only in the 50's! We're in the process of securing our temporary living quarters for when we arrive home June 17, so we got something important done. We'll secure an off-season furnished beachside apartment we found for a month while we look for a long-term place to rent in Florida.

The Parisians seem to start dinner about 6:00 for the early birds, but the main crowds flood in closer to 7:00. The Catalans in Barcelona eat dinner closer to 9 pm, no kidding, it's crazy. We're not the type who like to sit down for a two or three hour meal. We're Americans, dag nabbit, we got things to do. We'll prepare most of our meals in the apartment anyway and eat around 17:00 (5 pm).

So during many of these rain induced house arrests, I would saunter down to our mini lobby, say hello to Snowflake, then stand in our outdoor vestibule for great local people watching. I'd watch the locals driving their scooters in the rain wearing ponchos, and pedestrians soaked to the bone walking home from work carrying the traditional three-foot-long baguette.

Tonight at 6 pm, we were standing outside, and five fully armed soldiers patrolled by our lobby, and we are not in a tourist area? I've heard the American news say some unnerving things about Paris while we were here. We haven't witnessed any social upheaval or trouble at all. Next morning at 10 am, another five fully armed soldiers patrolled by in the rain. We use these soggy cold days to catch up on much needed rest.

We haven't been yelled at in any language since the cemetery picnic faux pas, so tomorrow we'll have to shake things up a little.

Cold and Rainy, to Notre Dame and Feeding Snowflake,
La Gentile Chat Blanc
Tuesday, May 31

Yucky, rainy, breezy, cold day again. When it's warmer in Michigan you know it's bad, but we gotta get out from these four walls. We bundled up and walked straight down Rue Monge (Rue = Street) to the end, and discovered it takes us right to Notre Dame, so we ducked inside again. Mass on Tuesdays, what's going on here, this has to stop, but they let us in anyway. With smaller crowds and slower pace, we soaked in the history and beauty of this charming basilica.

We were told Notre Dame fell into such great disrepair after the Revolution, there was serious talk about tearing her down. When Victor Hugo got wind of this, he wrote "The Hunchback of Notre Dame" to bring attention to her plight. The book became so popular, city officials decided instead to refurbish her.

On our way back to the apartment, we decided to pick Snowflake up some cat treats. She's such a sweetheart and the only local who'll make eye contact with us in Paris. Our local Franprix (grocery) doesn't have a big selection of pet supplies. They didn't carry cat treats, so we picked up a box of dry cat food. Entering our lobby, we tapped on the glass, and green eyes hopped up to greet us. We placed our goodies in front of her, and upon sniffing the gift we provided, she turned up her nose and became dismissive, even contemptuous, turning her back and walking away. Good thing she's behind that hockey glass, stupid Parisian cat. Later, just to humor us, she hopped up to the opening in the glass and forced down a few morsels. We made up and are good friends again. She's so cute and sweet, we can't stay mad at her for long.

Père Lachaise Cemetery
Paris, France

The grand stairway of L'Opera Garnier
Paris, France

Shakespeare and Company bookstore
Paris, France

Jardin des Plantis
Peaceful park near our apartment
Paris, France

185

Chapter 11

Sacré-Cœur

Exploring Sacré-Cœur Basilica in Montmartre, North Paris
Wednesday, June 1

Oh my God, only a 60% chance of rain today for two hours, we're out of here. We haven't seen the sun in days. We decided to be fancy people and take a cab today instead of the Metro. Rick Steves said a taxi would be about €15 to hitch a ride from the Seine to Sacré-Cœur, the artsy Montmartre section of Paris.

Taxi stands are everywhere, there's one three blocks from our place. We strutted up Rue Monge like VIP's, and asked the first taxi in line, "Combien au Sacré-Cœur?"

"Vingt-cinq."

I said, "Vingt-cinq?" with a graduated upswing in my tone, apparently forming a question in French. He went all crazy taxi driver on me, pointing to his meter, raising his voice in frustration.

"Desolee, c'est bon," so we climbed in, and off we went.

It's not quinze euros, it's vingt-cinq euros for a taxi; a difference of dix euros. However, the vingt-cinq euros we spent on this ride was better than the Rock and Roll roller coaster at Hollywood Studios. We were almost in three fatal accidents, twenty-two vehicular homicides, and watched scooter drivers do things on sidewalks you'd lose your license for back in the States. When we stepped out of the taxi, our faces were pale and hearts pounding.

Sacré-Cœur is on top of a hill, and it's massive. It reminds me of the Taj Mahal in color, posture, and design. It's gorgeous. This church is "newer" compared to most in the city; construction started in 1875 and dedicated in 1919. There's a brighter ambience inside this church. The light colored stone used in the construction brightens the inside of Sacré-Cœur, much more than inside Notre Dame, which is dark.

While walking on the inside of the church, pilgrims touched the feet of ole Saint Peter and blessed themselves for good luck. So many visitors have done this over the years that ole' Pete's toes on his right foot are almost gone. The ornate mosaics on the walls and ceiling were colorful and had bright gold details. While we were admiring inside the church, nuns were singing a cappella. When there's beautiful music in a special place it counts as a "moment", and this was one for us.

There's a real festive atmosphere on the steps of Sacré-Cœur. We were treated by a harpist playing Edith Piaf's "Le Vie En Rose" when we arrived, and later when we came out of the church, a young man with a guitar and small amplifier sang 90's hits. Two moments on the same steps, same day, I'm getting tingles! The singer beckoned to the audience to sing along. Most were unmoved, they just weren't into it. Looking at the crowd present, I surmised many of them weren't even born in the 90's or couldn't speak English.

Everywhere we go in Paris, we come across young asian couples, and only asian couples, having their wedding pictures taken at all the famous landmarks. So while they're posing and "in the moment" we take their picture. We're up to ten asian couples so far. Today there were two couples just at the steps at Sacré-Cœur being all newly wedded and stuff.

Legend has it during the dedication of the Sacré-Cœur Basilica, the owner of the Moulin Rouge ran up the hill screaming, "The devil is here, the devil is here!" Someone from the crowd yelled back at him, "No, the devil is down the hill!" (meaning his cabaret). I'm sorry, I'm not going to get in the middle of that one.

At many of these historic places, you will see "No Photo" signs, but what it really means is no flash photography. So Lis and I are walking with about 30 other tourists down the port side of Sacré-Cœur, and everyone is taking pictures (without flash).

Wouldn't you know it, this looney lady (who doesn't work at Sacré-Cœur) comes up to me, wags her crooked boney finger and says, "No pictures!" in her Transylvanian accent, and goes back to her pew and sits down. What the hell just happened? It was like the Twilight Zone. There were twenty-seven other people around us snapping away and still snapping away, and she said nothing to them. So, getting just a little indignant, I walked up and took a picture of her, Mrs. Looney Lady . . . . So I got reprimanded again or maybe cursed, I told you we were going to mix things up.

Montmartre, which means "Mountain of Mars", has a quiet hippy charm with its rolling hills and architecture. This area was not part of Paris until it was annexed in 1860. Montmartre was a gathering spot in the 1800's for struggling artists who would come and do their painter thingy. Picasso, Van Gogh, Renoir, and Toulouse-Lautrec used to hang out, paint, sip coffee, paint a little, get drunk, and talk artsy stuff.

From the church, we walked down the hill, past the old artist haunts, some of them preserved, others private, and others working establishments like Café des 2 Moulins and the Moulin Rouge. The Moulin de la Galette is where Renoir painted his famous "Dance at the Moulin Galette". His home, just around the corner, is fenced off, closed and a little overgrown.

We passed Van Gogh's house on the main road. One of Renoir's homes is a museum and his other home right down the street is a private residence.

Around the corner from Renoir's old home on Place Dalida is another famous pilgrimage site. The site is a bust of, you guessed it, Dalida. She is one of the world's most prolific singers and France's most popular female performer in history. She is ranked 6th as the most popular singer in the world of all time selling over 170 million records in ten different languages. Yeah, I never heard of her either, but we took a picture anyway.

The street Renoir lived on was hilly and picturesque with cobblestone roads, classic old homes, black ironwork, with vines growing up the stone walls. Rue Cortot sat all under the giant shadow of Sacré-Cœur. (Cover of the book)

Getting home via the Metro brought us back from the enchanting tourist world and back into reality. Heading down the steps at the Blanche Metro stop across from the Moulin Rouge to line 2, on line 2 for five stops to the Stalingrad (you heard me right) station, which is a major Metro hub, we continued for about a half mile through underground tunnels to our exchange train onto line 7.

While walking to board line 7, we came up to a split in the tunnel, and both directions had arrows going in opposite directions saying to line 7. We often had confusing signage in France, so we stood there bemused until we realized one arrow was for steps and the other was for escalators. We took line 7 for sixteen stops back to Place Monge. The cab took twenty-five minutes and a year off our lives for €21, and the Metro took about thirty-five minutes for €2.80 for both of us.

Some entrepreneur thought it would be a good idea to offer what is known as a Museum Pass for the cherished visitors to Paris. In order to ease anxiety for their customers, they made it so you had to cram your two, four or six-day passes in consecutive days. They don't have three or five-day passes, no, that would make too much sense. So grandma and grandpa, who are only here for a week, will have to jam four to eight museums into four consecutive days, not taking into account the rain, snow, sleet, flooding, transit strikes, broken ankles, or hospitalizations.

Things we can learn from the French: There are no overhead electric wires cluttering the view, everything is underground, so no unsightly wires. Wide streets and thoroughfares, thanks to Napoleon who wanted the ability to fire his cannons at civilians in case of another revolution, merci beaucoup Napoleon. The museums are reasonably priced for the unwashed masses. Paris and Nice have a great city bike rental program for short-term rides. They've maintained their historic buildings beautifully. The French police seem more tolerant, and allow for more creative driving than in the States, especially for motorbikes. You can get anywhere on public transportation, and most of the time for as low as €1.40. There are bakeries (patisseries) on every corner. Paris doesn't feel like a congested city. Most of the cities we visited have huge parks and gardens. The old architecture is spectacular, grand, and "get the hell out of here beautiful", in that order. A simple doctor visit with medicine cost under €50. The groceries are reasonably priced, no need to hunt for coupons or major sales. Kids are well-behaved and operate at a much lower volume. Most people dress classy to classy comfortable, no white sneakers. :(Last but not least, they speak French beautifully.

While relaxing in our room for the weather to clear up (which might take till August), we found a scale in the bathroom. Let's see what we weigh in kilos? It was great, 1 kilo is about 2 pounds, so we weighed half of our normal weight. I haven't seen those numbers in pounds for a couple decades, so we're in a great mood!

RAIN Again! Explore Nearby Roman Arena and Mosque
Thursday, June 2

June 2nd and the high was 56, cold, damp, rain, and clouds, no sun. I think it was warmer during the real battle of Stalingrad. The weatherman has been wrong here all week: zero chance of rain today, and it rained all day. Last week it was a 70% chance of rain, and it was beautiful and sunny.

Today we bundled up and ambled up Rue Monge to our own mini Roman amphitheater. There's not much left, just the oval outline and one wall. After a quick little tour, it's down the road to the Grand Mosque. We didn't get to see the whole Mosque last time, because we were tossed out. As we neared the mosque, we were approached by a guy twenty years younger, better health and better dressed, asking me for money . . . . Yeahhhh nooooooo! After we refused to contribute to his chic designer clothes addiction, he gave us the ole entitled beggar's stink eye.

Inside the mosque, near (but not in) the prayer room, a young man walked up to Lis and barked something to her in Arabic. Let me tell you, it was not in a complimentary tone. Lis was the only female visitor covering her head with the hood of her jacket out of respect. She was also covered head to toe (since it was a cold day), so we have no idea what it was about. How did he know we were infidels?

Our cheeky encounter wasn't about taking pictures, since they didn't have a sign prohibiting it and other visitors were snapping away. Everyone else in the Grand Mosque were hospitable and welcoming, so we didn't let it color our experience. The place was beautiful and an enriching cultural experience.

After resting and drying out at our apartment, we headed to the Seine River to check out the flooding from all the rain. We're really learning how to take advantage of the Velib bike rental system. We biked downhill to the river. It's a lot higher than yesterday, completely flooding the walkways, but not the retaining walls along the river. The U.S. World News made it apocalyptic of course, but the locals took it all in stride.

Another Rainy Day, Seine River Really Flooding
Friday, June 3

Well, the forecast stated it was only supposed to be cloudy today, so we did a little "Yippee!" and headed out again on bikes to see the Seine River, it's supposed to crest today at 17 meters. As we got on the Velib bikes to head down to the Seine, it started the now all too familiar cold, light drizzle, ugh! The high today is 57, in frigging June???? Pour l'amour de Dieu! (For the love of God!)

The Seine River rose a lot higher since yesterday. The water taxi ticket kiosk we used to purchase our tickets last week is halfway under water. The river is about twenty feet wider than it was last week. The hard rain in other parts of France and Germany has contributed to the flooding here. The local news reported the Loire Valley outside of Paris was also flooded. The Loire Valley was supposed to be our next scheduled stop after Paris.

All of the walkways and trails along the Seine are underwater and roped off. The "C" train line that travels along the Seine is below ground level, leaking water, and therefore closed. Flood water cascaded down the outside retaining walls onto the exposed train tracks. This is the train which takes tourists to Versailles, so we hope this train is back up and running soon so we can go to this king-sized attraction. We have been anxiously waiting and hoping for the weather to clear for an extended time so we can use the Museum Pass efficiently.

The main reason to get the Museum Pass is #1 Versailles, the cost of the Pass almost covers entrance fees at the palace. #2 The Louvre, because you can avoid the incredibly long lines to get in. #3 It covers entrance fees and ticket lines for many more attractions. We need a sunny day for Versailles, and would like to have a couple decent days for traversing Paris to get to the other museums covered by the Pass.

Half of the day at Versailles is exploring the huge king-sized gardens, so we'd like to be out of the rain and cold. Hopefully later in the week we will see the sun in the near forecast and have some hope, ugh!

Lis and I rode our bikes down along the Seine to Notre Dame. Along the way, locals tried desperately to secure their boats along the river's edge. Two enormous restaurant barges were dangerously close to contacting one of the ornate bridges, and their ropes appeared to be fraying.

All of the maintenance buildings along the river walkways are halfway submerged. At this time, the river is flowing faster than we've ever seen it. The water is so high, the only thing that can sail under the bridges are really small ducks.

Due to the lack of clearance under the bridges, the water taxis are shut down today. The water is about eight to ten feet higher than normal levels and three feet higher than yesterday. Trees and street lamps along the walkways appear to be standing in the middle of the river. Parisians and tourists were taking pictures and selfies (of course, always with the selfies) against the back drop of this once in a lifetime flood.

We are witnessing a 100-year flood! The last time the Seine flooded this bad was in 1910, the water reached a height of 28 meters. Today the water was at the 15-17 meters mark, which isn't as bad as 28, but still unnerving. The Louvre closed today so it could move its lower level artwork to upper floors. The Mona Lisa is in a safe upper level. I don't know when the Louvre will reopen, hopefully soon, because we were planning on going back to see the two sections we missed the first time, the Denon and Sully wings.

These closings and bad weather are really messing with our timing for using the stupid Museum Pass. Other than skipping the lines at the Louvre and Rodin museum, I really regret buying the Museum Pass. The anxiety with timing combined with bad weather are just a pain in the arts. I can't imagine the angst for those who only had a short time to use it. They'd have to go to Versailles in the rain.

The Musée d'Orsay and the Louvre practiced emergency flooding drills a couple months ago. The employees rehearsed moving lower level pieces of art to higher places. It took a few days to complete, and now they have to do it again.

Parking our bikes in St. Germain, we walked around Notre Dame to take pictures of the reliefs up close. They are stunning, such beautiful detail, the time and workmanship are amazing. It was disgusting to see the sculptures on the northern street side of the church damaged and with missing pieces. Much of the damage happened during the enlightened "Revolution". A tall iron fence protects the damaged side of the church. The Seine side of Our Lady doesn't seem to have much damage.

Continuing behind Notre Dame, we observed pickpockets busy at their seedy craft. Young gypsy ladies pose as petition gatherers, and were working a middle-aged couple big time. We tried to warn the lady they were scammers and pickpockets, but she couldn't understand English or wouldn't listen. These two scammers actually convinced the target to give them a donation along with their signature. When the target pulled out and opened her wallet, the gypsies eyes swelled and other operatives appeared from nowhere, moving in quickly like water bugs, hands flying, confusion, and poof, they disappeared like cockroaches into different directions. I'm not sure they stole anything. There were just too many hands for me to follow.

Wanting to explore the Île Saint-Louis, it started raining again, in the all too familiar cold, damp rain. We're Floridians, and Paris spring showers just chill us to the bone. We grabbed the Velib rental bikes and peddled our way back uphill to the apartment, looking like drowned rats. We actually wore hats and gloves today to stay warm, it's mid-day in June! Lis is deathly afraid of getting sick again, five weeks was long enough, so we have to be careful.

Plodding home, we were again greeted by the beautiful green-eyed Snowflake. She looked at us as if to say, "Only a dog would be out in that weather?" And she was right! We dried off, and after resting a bit, I went next door to pick up some groceries.

On the way out of the lobby, I left Snowflake some cat treats, but she acted coy and uninterested again, so I just left them. When I came back from the grocery, the treats were gone, and she was napping. Green eyes is definitely a Parisian cat!

Okay, Lis has to confess, she is addicted to Parisian candy. We purchased a bag of Haribo Dragibus, tart, multicolored jellybeans in our grocery store. Here they cost around €1.50. On Amazon in the U.S. they're $13, so you can guess what's coming home in our luggage. The high cost must be the big shipping expense from France to the U.S.?

We've also developed a minor addiction to these jelly cookies from Franprix, called "Tartelettes". A container of twelve cookies is only €.49, and they are good!!! When I bring these cookies home, Lis is smiling like the butcher's dog.

We hope to stay dry, warm, and healthy this week! Maybe, just maybe we will see the sun before we leave for home! I do complain a lot about the weather, but when the sun comes out, even for an hour, Paris is the most incredible city I could ever imagine.

Long distance view of the city of Paris from the hill of Montmartre
Paris, France

Montmartre street scene
Paris, France

Montmartre street scene
Paris, France

June 3, 2016 Flood water levels
Seine River, Paris, France

Chapter 12

Arc de Triomphe and Lady Diana's Memorial

Arc de Triomphe, Lady Diana's Memorial, Outside of the Louvre

Samedi, 4 Juin 2016

Saturday morning was cold and damp with a sprinkle of rain. The weatherman here has been missing the mark so far. We've wanted to get to the Arc de Triomphe the last four days, but you really need decent weather because, well, it's outside. It's a good thing we're here for a month.

The sun was hiding, so we headed out a little late, about 11:45, hopped on our Metro line for six stops to the Louvre, exchanged trains, then another four stops on line 1 to the Franklin Roosevelt station on the Champs-Élysées. From the exit, we were now only six city blocks from the Arc. We probably could have waited one more stop on the Metro, but getting off where we did gave us the awe of seeing the colossus grow as we approached. Holy moly, it's "gihunormousamungous". All of these famous monuments are way bigger in person than they appear in pictures.

The Champs-Élysées, it's packed with tourists, entitled rich people with miniature entitled dogs, and gobs of asians doing silly poses in front of the chic boutiques and popular monuments. It's great people watching here!

Underneath the Arc is a pedestrian tunnel which runs underneath Place Charles de Gaulle circle where over-caffeinated French drivers merge from twelve different streets. Without this tunnel, I would estimate a minimal three hundred tourists a day would die there. Considering our options, we decided to use the tunnel and popped right up next to the monument. We're standing right next to the Arc de Triomphe. It truly is surreal.

The 3D artwork on the face of the Arc is just dramatic. The reliefs conjure up feelings of patriotism and courage, and I'm not even French. Lis used up about a terabyte on the external hard drive for her pictures here.

While standing admiring the Arch, a middle-aged gypsy guy tried the old "Did you drop that gold ring?" trick on me. It's really a copper ring, one of many he carries in his pocket. Being the nice guy he is, he'll let you keep the ring, but would appreciate a small finder's fee. He also happens to know the spot price on gold for the day. I shooed him away. After twenty minutes, the same guy hit me up again. "Hey, pal, I may be Irish, but I'm not stupid, hit the road."

Oh, yeah, I'd have to say this, at the Arc de Triomphe, which is in the middle of Place Charles de Gaulle, is a giant 12 lane traffic circle, like the ones they have all over New Jersey. Get this, the drivers entering the circle have the right of way, and those inside have to yield. Boy oh boy, it's crazy to watch, with lots of horn beeping, and cursing. This was one of our many head-shaking "what the hell" moments you'll find in Paris.

Napoleon commissioned this 164 foot Arc in 1806 and displayed the names of his loyal generals and winning battles. On the face of the arch, Napoleon hand-picked four battle scene sculptural groups and six reliefs. At the foundation of the Arc de Triomphe is their eternal flame for all the young boys who died in WW1. The eternal flame here was the inspiration Jackie Kennedy used in the design of her husband's grave in Arlington National Cemetery.

An enormous French flag that appeared to be two stories wide and four stories tall hung inside the arch and waved with the breeze. When the wind blew hard the scene was simply dramatic.

While sitting and admiring this colossus, two young ladies from Boston asked if we could take their picture, and afterwards we chatted a spell. What a couple of sweet peas, it was great to converse in American English for a time. I'm encouraged to see young people traveling; I wish I'd done more when I was younger.

This open-ended odyssey we're on will help make up for some of my lost travel adventures.

Since the flooded Seine River is on national news, we headed back down to see the old girl. We figured on grabbing two of those Velib rental bikes and cruise the nine blocks downhill to the water, easy, right? The only rental station we could find had two bikes, and one had a chain off. I couldn't fix the chain, it seems to have been designed as to not allow customers to work on the things. We ended up walking the nine blocks. Our new shoes we bought for this trip are starting to look old and worn.

Walking down Ave Marceau, we finally made it to the Seine, hung a Louis XIV (left), and we came up to an underground auto tunnel that goes below the intersection at the Pont de l'Alma bridge. "Lis, this looks like the place where Lady Di had her car accident," and it was. Above the tunnel on the sidewalk was the Flamme de la Liberté, a torch sculpture which looks like a copy of one the Statue of Liberty holds. Lis was an admirer of the princess, being she (Lis) lived in London, England as a child. The memorial was adorned with various pictures of Lady Diana and multiple bouquets of fresh cut flowers. Sorry to report that shamelessly there were corporate sponsors carved into the marble monument. Come on fellas, stay classy, try to stay classy, please.

As we walked along the river, we noticed the Eiffel Tower had a huge soccer ball hanging from the center. We heard of an international soccer tournament being played in Paris, but we're not sure, it's soccer and we're Americans.

The Lady Di memorial and the Louvre are only about six blocks from one another, and we needed to walk that way to get home. Even though the Louvre was closed today due to the flooding, you could still wander around and appreciate the outside, and as always, great people watching. The Louvre has enough stunning architecture to last you a few days just walking around the outside. Did a lot of walking and biking today, and were rewarded with about fifteen whole minutes of unrelenting sunshine, yeah!

St. Germain Area, Sorbonne, Cluny Museum, Panthéon, and Notre Dame to See Seine River Receding
Sunday, June 5

We decided to take it easy and bike down to the St. Germain section because of the good write-ups and a couple things we wanted to see. Up Rue Monge to the bike rack, punch in our super secret numbers, disconnect our bikes from the dock, and off we went. I forgot to inspect my bike and ended up with a wobbly front wheel and needed to take it slow. We biked down Rue Lacépède towards the Seine, and instead of passing by the park as usual, we turned left in front of it and ditty bopped about eight blocks to the Sorbonne, which is the big ivy league level school of France. Many a French big wig and future leaders attend here. Not a whole lot to see there at the school, we couldn't go in.

Across the street from the front of the Sorbonne, we found the Musée de Cluny, a smaller medieval-looking building which houses antiquities from Roman times. We'll put Cluny on our B list to see later, it's covered with the Museum Pass.

The third and final location we wanted to experience today is the Panthéon, which we just found out is pretty close to our apartment in our 5th arrondissement. The Panthéon is an enormous edifice dedicated to the "Enlightenment"; it's like a church for humanists. The facade contained most of the external gingerbread: nineteen enormous Corinthian columns, five reliefs, and a twenty-four foot tall front door modeled after the Pantheon in Rome. Quite a few of the big wigs of the Enlightenment are entombed here: Voltaire, Rousseau, Victor Hugo, Emile Zola, Moulin, Braille, Jaures, and Soufflot. The place had a cross on top, which made it really confusing to me. We will be back to go inside, during the big Museum Pass squeeze.

We desperately looked for a bike stand on Rue Saint Jacque by the Panthéon, but they were as rare as a public bathroom on this day, so we walked toward the now visible Eiffel Tower. As we neared the Seine off to our right, a throng of tourists milled about, so we joined in the crowd.

As we meandered past the trendy cafes on this old St. Germain street, we beheld one of the most beautiful sights in all of Paris. Not the Mona Lisa, Venus de Milo, Sacré-Cœur, Alexander Bridge, Musée d'Orsay; no, a breathtaking, exquisite Algerian pastry shop window. Who needs the Mona Lisa, we drooled at the window for a good five minutes along with a couple British ladies. Some people even took selfies in front of the window. Sullen, we had to leave for lunch, we promised those beautiful visions we'd be back soon, real soon. The pastries, not the British ladies!

Five doors down from the most heavenly of sights, we found a Spanish restaurant with thousands of currency notes from all over the world taped to one another on the walls. "Cool vibe," so we stopped in for soup; it was a soupy kind of a day after all. After lunch, Lis tried to pay with a 10 billion dollar Zimbabwe note and still came up short. No, we did not steal any money off the wall, that would be silly.

Sixteen euros for two bowls of mediocre soup is why 90% of our meals are made at home. I see why the French mostly order a shot glass of expresso and sit at the outside tables for two or three hours and la chit la chat.

Remembering our promise to those sweeties, we made a beeline back to the Algerian patisserie and walked into what can only be described as heaven's welcoming lobby. Wall to wall, floor to ceiling of the most beautiful gut-busting delights this side of heaven. We purchased three baklava wedges: one for me, one for Lis, and one for me. They were nutty, buttery, flakey, honey sweet, and Y-U-M-M-Y.

Though this probably annoys the locals, the lingua franca in France is English. And since we're pretty good with English, we can talk to almost anyone, even the Algerian bakers. Once at a bus stop in Èze, a Swedish girl conversed with an Italian girl in English. It's a good thing I paid attention in English class.

Fueled up on a sugar high, we walked down to Notre Dame, which we ashamedly take for granted now. We've been here so many times, if I were Catholic, I'd consider Notre Dame my home church. We hung around the basilica to watch the bright-eyed and bushy-tailed baby tourists for about an hour. They're so cute at that age. People from all over the world come here to see the beauty that is Paris. Bus #47 was right across the street, so when we were ready, we just hopped on for a ten-minute sardine-like ride back to our place.

I swear when we get on a crowded bus, it appears at each stop only one person gets off and ten get on. It can get extremely claustrophobic quickly at times. Lis always informs the people blocking the door in English, she's getting off at the next stop. The veteran passenger usually answers her with a reassuring nod as if to say, "Yes, everything will be alright."

We took about three hundred pictures between the two of us today, so it's home for a little rest. After a fifty-minute cat nap, our batteries recharged anew, it's down to the Seine to witness the flooding which has made world news back home. Today it looks like the waters receded about two feet from yesterday. The river is still attracting a lot of curious Parisians and tourists alike.

At Pont au Change, the bridge with the large letter "N" fashioned on its face ("N" for Napoleon), the water was flowing inches below the "N" crest. I've heard from the locals, if the Seine waters should reach the "N" on a full moon, Napoleon will rise from the dead, take control of the Grande Armée, rescue France over from today's politicians, and look out Europe, it's payback time. Yeah, I'm not really sure about that one?

La Palais Royal, Outside of Louvre Again, Fire at the Louvre
Monday, June 6

Taking it easy today to rest up for the upcoming big Museum Pass squeeze, we'll be squeezing as many museums into our 4 day Pass we can without dying. Our easy day starts with a casual bike ride down to the swollen river, up past Notre Dame, over to and through the Louvre courtyard, to the Rue de Pyramids.

A block up the Rue de Pyramids, we found the Paris City Tours office so Lis can secure her ticket for Saturday's excursion to Giverny. Giverny is Monet's garden and house an hour west of Paris. It was difficult to find a Velib bike stand to park, so we headed back to the Louvre where we returned the bikes and walked. We surpassed the half hour limit and incurred a whopping €1 penalty for each bike.

Across from the Louvre at the famous "#PARIS WE LOVE YOU" sign, there is a complex known as La Palais Royal. The Palace is a quintessential 17th century French structure. It's a local hangout surrounding a park with working fountains, tree sculpted tunnel, and of course cafes. We relaxed and snacked like locals by the fountain on this beautiful sunny afternoon.

After a little walk back through the Louvre and about 200 pictures later, we crossed the Pont Neuf bridge (New Bridge), and flames were coming from in front of the Louvre. The smoke was black and billowing. We grabbed some rental bikes and headed toward the fire, but it was on the other side of the river, so we perched by the banks. It looked like a car in flames to us. The fire may have been partially inside one of the tunnels that allows you inside the courtyards, so it looked pretty bad. Even the locals seemed a little concerned.

It's not easy getting back home by bike when you head home against traffic. Along the Seine are wide sidewalks, but with the vendors, tourists, and locals it just isn't wide enough sometimes. Many pedestrians here don't even consider oncoming bikes. They will sometimes step right into the bike lane just as you approach. I had to swerve too many times the month we were in Paris.

Exhausted, we made it to the lobby and no kitty cat today, sometimes she's there, other times she's not. She's an enigma wrapped in catnip sometimes. We have no idea who owns Snowflake, as we've never seen anyone with her. Perhaps a cleaning person brings her to work or she's from one of the upstairs apartments. We just don't know. So it's up to our palatial one room apartment for a little snooze. Tomorrow is the big day.

Arc de Triomphe
Paris, France

Panthéon
Paris, France

The Algerian Bakery in the St. Germain section
Paris, France

St. Denis holding his head at the entrance of Notre Dame
Paris, France

The Pont au Change bridge ("N" for Napoleon), during the Seine River flooding
Paris, France

Bouquinistes selling used books along the Seine River
Paris, France

Chapter 13

The Big Super Squeeze Museum Pass Days!

Sainte-Chapelle, Conciergerie, Rodin Museum, Panthéon

Tuesday, June 7

A beautiful day finally, and we're starting the big squeeze. Our plan was to visit Sainte-Chapelle (I call it Dave Chappell) and the Conciergerie, then it depends how we feel.

It's not unusual in the Metro for musicians to just jump in a car and start playing their instruments. Today, a father and son trumpet team graced us with their presence.

The first song we were treated to was a lovely harmonic duet, delightful and surprisingly not as loud as you would expect in such a confined space. The second "song" was a different story; the matrix started to crack, evil entered the realm. The duet fell apart, they screeched as if someone pulled a cat through their trumpet, sorry Snowflake. It's as if these two gentlemen were playing two completely different songs and never noticed. It was sensory torture, maybe that was the plan, I wanted to pay them to stop. Two old Frenchmen sitting near us shook their heads, commented to each other, and smiled. We couldn't understand what they were saying, but their body language said it all.

The Conciergerie, which is one of the main structures on the Île de la Cité, started its life as the hall of justice (courthouse), and in 1793 it became the holding cells for those condemned to die by guillotine after the "Enlightenment" and during the "Reign of Terror", including Marie Antoinette.

Sainte-Chapelle, a Gothic royal chapel from 1248, is tucked away behind a working government building and thus a little hard to find. It's a smaller church, but beautiful as is all their older architecture. Once inside, you find a somewhat unimpressive lower chapel, only to realize later, the main area of the church was overhead. We had to locate and ascend thirty-three very narrow steps in a dark spiral staircase. I used my smartphone to light the way. From the darkness, you enter the sanctuary with its colored light from the enormous amount of stained glass windows. Sainte-Chapelle wasn't as well-known or prestigious, but it was worth it.

To find the Conciergerie, we filtered out of the church, back through the immense iron entrance gate, down a half block, and without signage to guide us, we entered an unassuming door and found it. We passed through more security, hoping Lisa's jelly beans would clear any hungry inspectors.

The fortress appears as if it was built yesterday. It's hard to believe this structure is from the 1600's. As we toured the multi-arched, artistically lit interior, we came upon Marie Antoinette's cell and the rooms where other prisoners were housed. The conditions were similar to a hotel. You had to pay for any upgrades, a cot, table, food, bowl of water, and blankets, et al, just like a hotel except they killed you when your stay is over. The Conciergerie was full of royal governmental history and impressive architecture, but I'd put it in our B list of things to see.

With two museums down and still having plenty energy, I said to Lis, "Let's rent bikes and hit the Musée d'Orsay, we can see it now and free up some time in another day." It was 11:30, and the day is young. Surmising from our maps, the Musée d'Orsay seemed just a couple blocks away, we walked instead of biked. Lesson learned, always opt for bikes even when it appears on the map to be close. After another half hour walk on hard pavement, I'm exhausted. Did I say it hit 84 degrees today? Guess what, d'Orsay is closed, and no one in La Organization thought it would be a good idea to put this fact on their website, EGH!

Due to museum officials' oversight, there are around two hundred stranded asian tourists in front of Musée d'Orsay, desperately pecking away on their phones, looking for other options.

According to the map, it appears we are six blocks from the Rodin Museum. We could hit that quick and finish the last two thirds of the Armée Museum. They are just a few blocks from each other. Saying goodbye to our new stranded Chinese friends, we walked all of fifteen more blocks, and the Museum Pass pays off. Strutting in like VIP's, we skip right to the front of the line and flew right through security. Like the tiny, listless Mona Lisa, I don't get clunky Rodin, but who am I? After two hours of trying to figure out why I'm here, I became too fatigued to continue on and finish the last two thirds of the Armée Museum from two weeks ago. I was exhausted. We should have used bikes to get here.

It's time to close up the gang box, head home to rest up for tomorrow's second venture inside the Louvre. We've hung outside the Louvre so many times now, I think the cops are getting suspicious.

So it's home, and after a Snowflake-like catnap and dinner, we decided to shoot up Rue Lacépède and experience the inside of the Panthéon. With the sun still shining bright, we biked uphill about six blocks, and glancing to our right, out from amongst all the other apartment buildings, there it is, and like everything else here, it's gigantic.

The Panthéon, first built as a church, is today a mausoleum to the heroes of the Enlightenment. Those that disagreed with the Enlightenment were buried elsewhere in less prestigious memorials. The victors do write the history books and build the giant memorials like this one. The building is quite impressive inside.

The inside was breathtaking with the history of the Enlightenment in statues, paintings and reliefs. The carvings, the details, the amount of artistry is mind-boggling.

Finding the spiral stairway down, we ventured into the crypt. The ceilings were stylish, arched and higher than I'd expect for a place that stored the dead. Effect lighting lit our way, hidden lamps pointed upward toward the ceiling, and the light-colored stone walls illuminated the way. Straight ahead was a main hallway with branches that broke off and contained rooms with multiple crypts with the names and dates of the occupants. Voltaire seems to be the "big man on campus" here and was honored with a life-sized statue in a prominent area. Overall, we enjoyed this place, the architecture was breathtaking.

Inside the Louvre Second Time
Wednesday, June 8

On the first rainless day after the great deluge, with Museum Pass in hand, and it's off to the Metro. Six now very familiar stops to the Louvre. Our Museum Pass rewarded us big time with a no line, secret entrance at the Richelieu wing.

Skating right through security, down an escalator, and bada bing we're in. It's on to the Denon wing and the other half of Sully.

While experiencing tons of very remarkable artwork, we turn a corner, then bam, in the distance, Winged Victory; down a grand arched hallway bathed in natural light, surrounded by a swarming crowd of selfie-taking tourists. A headless, armless Greek statue perched on the bow of a ship. A lot of theories abound, but it's not clear of her meanings.

After another short walk, admiring all the beautiful artwork, some we recognize. Then with absolutely no warning, there's the Mona Lisa with the biggest, most obnoxious crowd, pushing and shoving to position themselves for the perfect selfie with Mrs. Lisa. Sorry, I don't get the stamp-sized Mona Lisa or Winged Victory thing. They must have a great PR firm on their payroll. As for "getting" the Venus de Milo mystique, I don't. We passed twenty other beautiful Greek marble statues complete with arms right down the hall from her that are stunning?

I really liked the paintings by David, all the Egyptian booty, the friezes and statues from Persia, Nineveh, and Mesopotamia. Lis loved Napoleon III's apartment. She appreciated the detailed paintings, the architecture, and fancy doors. All the while you're walking these marble floors, you keep thinking, "OMG, I'm in the Louvre, I can't freaking believe we're here?"

The Louvre can be painfully frustrating to navigate. It's poorly marked, the levels are labeled on the map -2, -1, 0, 1, 2. You can tell it was built in sections over a long period of time. Many throughways were closed, so you can't just scoot across the entire floor, no, that would be British, don't you know? Sometimes you have to walk up a floor, across, and back down to continue along the way.

There seems to be an underlying contrarian attitude here in Paris, the number one most visited city in the world, and things are poorly marked. This museum is the size of a small Bavarian state and has only one exit (not including the Metro). Getting to the exit takes a huge effort from the outside end of a wing. Up and down steps through unmarked hallways, and you pass one hundred locked exit doors to the outside. It felt like Dr. Evil's cruel labyrinth at times, when you could see freedom through glass doors, but still had a mile to walk for freedom.

Versailles, Walking Champs-Élysées, Orangerie Museum
Thursday, June 9

The big day to Versailles. We met a delightful couple from New York around our age while we were in line at the Conciergerie. After chatting a spell, we agreed to split a cab for the forty-five minute ride to Versailles. The RER C train line was flooded, and the conductors were on strike. I know, a strike in France, who would have thunk it?

We met Joe and Dana in the morning at the Charlemagne statue in front of Notre Dame. We walked a block toward St. Germain and found the stand with taxis. Going to the front of the line, our driver looked like he could have been from Tahiti and didn't speak a lick of the Queen's English, but he understood "Versailles". He smiled and nodded, we got in, and off we went.

Door to door service, no Metro, trumpet players, pickpockets, steps or gypsies. Louis the XIV here we come! Had a nice ride out into the country with our new compatriots from New York. We hit it off like long lost friends. Who could have imagined a Giants and an Eagles fan sharing a cab? He dropped us off right at the main gate to Versailles, and not to sound too repetitive, it's enormous.

To be honest with you, Versailles was a little disappointing, especially after being in the Louvre. You can remove all the art at the Louvre, and the building is still worth the price of admission. Versailles' uniqueness was its size, the expanse of both building and gardens were unbelievable. The Louvre was strong and majestic, Versailles, grand and glitzy. Both were incredible.

They say Versailles was built on swamp land, so the engineers needed to move an unbelievable amount of earth. It sits atop a graded stretch of land that extends downhill about five futbol (soccer) pitches to a small lake. This was all at a time before bulldozers?

The inside was typical Louis XIV with audacious architectural touches: gold leafed alabaster carvings, terrazzo pillars, marble statues, mirrors, cornices, Baroque art on walls and ceilings, polished brass and woods. Enormous building, enormous grounds and enormous ego is the theme here. It really makes for a grand statement.

There can't be anyone left in China; there are so many Chinese here in Paris. We love the Chinese young people on our cruise, but in a crowd, when the adults hit critical mass, something happens, something aggressive, something primal. When a Chinese tour comes into a confined area, they take over, it's every man for himself and to hell with everyone else. It can be very unpleasant. Negative articles have been written in the local papers about the Chinese tourist.

The gardens at Versailles were massive, but lacking flowers and color this time of year. Lis liked the topiaries, fountains, and sculptures, which added a lot of interest. Only one fountain was on briefly, a huge modern vertical monolith at least five stories tall and emptied into a huge pool at the back of the garden. It gave the appearance of a waterfall suspended in mid-air when it was running.

Versailles was originally designed with 1500 fountains, now there are a measly 300. On Tuesdays they put on a fountain show, but it's Thursday, so "No show for us." On a whole, Lis and I were a little disappointed with Versailles; the Louvre, La Petit Palais, and the Opera were more opulent pertaining to the art and architecture, although Versailles was quite palatial. C'est la vie, non regrette. (That's life, no regrets.)

At the taxi stand outside the main gate, we met a couple ladies from California who were also going back to Notre Dame. We split a hard to find cab three ways (Joe and Dana were still there), and it went smoothly. Everybody behaved themselves and didn't bring up politics. Lis and I faced backwards in the van, so our blood pressure was fine. We didn't have to watch the "creative, ambitious" driving.

As we entered the city, our cabbie informed us of a traffic jam near Notre Dame, so he dropped us off at the Arc de Triomphe. From the Arc, we walked the entire Champs-Élysées to the L'Orangerie Museum 1.3 miles away.

The Orangerie contains several giant waterlily paintings Monet made near the end of his life. These unique paintings were done just for the opening of this museum. Downstairs exhibited other works by Renoir, Cézanne, Matisse, Picasso, and Braque. It was an honor seeing these paintings up close and in person.

Lis's favorite artists are Monet and Renoir. Her favorite painting by Monet in this museum was "Argentuil", a bright multicolored masterpiece centered around two red sailboats anchored in a lake. After two and a half hours on marble floors, my joints were screaming and gas tank was completely empty. It's running down earlier and earlier each passing day, and we still have to move our stuff out of storage when we get home to Florida, egh.

Bus 24 to LaGrange, off and grab a Velib bike, peddle uphill to home, exhausted, Advil, nap, amen.

Musée d'Orsay
Friday, June 10

Our only goal today is the crown jewel, the Musée d'Orsay, on the Seine with the Museum Pass. After a bowl of Petals and coffee, we're out the door and down to the lobby. We rode our bikes down to Gare Austerlitz, and hopped on Bus 24 toward the old town. Bus 24 from Gare Austerlitz was another one of those surprise, arrête-toi or "get the hell out" rides I mentioned before. We got off and waited another 6 minutes for another Bus 24 to finish our trek to the museum. We arrived at the museum around 11:00 am. It's an enormous, gorgeous, renovated old railroad station, pound for pound, inch for inch arguably the most beautiful building in Paris.

D'Orsay, a former railroad station hub, is one of the majestic buildings along the Seine. It's a behemoth structure facing the river, with it's two enormous clocks, lavish cornices and flowing alabaster carvings. D'Orsay sets the stage and ambience for anyone traveling along the river.

D'Orsay was closed down by the latest record-breaking deluge, but she's back and ready to roll. Through security and into the lobby, she's massive inside with hundreds of 3D flower crested ceiling ornaments framed in sage green, and impressive old windows lighting up the grand expanse.

Monet, Manet, Pissarro, Seurat, Guillaumin, Sully, Renoir, Van Gogh, Cassatt, all the big boys are here and in mass. We had a set of Van Gogh coasters in our apartment, and today we stood in front of the originals, yeah!

I have to tell you this, when you first walk into this enormous building, the major impressionists are on the 5th floor. If you want to start topside and walk down . . . welllll, the architects have you immediately walking up five flights of stairs right next to escalators going down. Yeah, that's right, stairs up, escalators down. Let that sink in, are you kidding me? Welcome to France! If you walk to the far end of the museum, you'll find escalators going up and stairs going down, but it's not obvious on the tourist maps.

D'Orsay closed the entire Georges Seurat section, and this was the artist we really wanted to see. We inquired at the "Information Desk" as to what "temporarily closed" means?

"I don't know," she said.

"Why is half the museum closed?"

"I don't know."

"This is the information desk, right?"

She answered me with a smirk and shoulder shrug. I shook my head and thought, *"Absolutely no information at the information desk. I swear this feels like a Seinfeld episode or Bizarro World?"*

The incredible beauty of d'Orsay doesn't allow one to stay miffed too long, come on, I'm in Paris. The building, the sculptures, and paintings are out of this world. I like this place better than the Louvre. It's smaller, better layout and everything is easy to find. You can even put your face right up to an original Masterpiece, and no one gets upset. It's such an honor to be here!

At the fifth floor lounge, there was a choice to recline on a giant hand-shaped couch or an enormous nine person circular beast and gaze through the giant see-through clock at the city landscape. While I was comfortably recovering by myself on the pie-shaped couch, a large group of high school age tourists clamored into the lobby, and all rushed to get onto the giant hand. However, one of the stragglers, a young lady full of innocent youthful energy, ran straight toward me, and with the tenacity of an Olympic high jumper, leaped to an Olympic height of around 5 feet. Lifting her feet parallel with the ground, she landed deadweight on the seat right next to me. Even though the sections were divided by armrests, it was still one giant connected bubble. Miss high jumper landed with so much force, the bubble inside the cushion almost launched me off the couch. I don't think she realized what she had done, she was too busy giggling to her friend and texting. It was just too cute and innocent to get upset.

After walking up and viewing the 5th (top) floor of impressionists, we moseyed out onto the balcony for one of the most spectacular 180 degree panoramic views of the city. My favorite church, Sacré-Cœur, is the centerpiece of this gorgeous Right Bank skyline. The museum has a food cart on the roof of d'Orsay, so we each enjoyed a poulet baguette sandwich and drink in the beautiful sunshine, I'd say a wonderful moment. From the roof, we could also see the Seine River right below, the Louvre, and the Opera in the distance. I really don't need to wait in line and climb up the claustrophobic steps of Notre Dame now with this view. We hung out for a while and just soaked it all in.

Back inside, we viewed the big boys of impressionism, realism, and sculpture; you really have to pinch yourself. I'm getting so much culture in this place, I might be turning into yogurt.

After d'Orsay, we tried to get into a small military museum right next door, but it was closed. TripAdvisor commenters said they open when they want and close when they're not in the mood, so we went with the flow and moved on.

After our failed attempt at the military museum, we decided to call it a day. While walking to find a bike station, I said, "This is the first time we are going home without being on the edge of death by exhaustion, and that was nice." We biked home for a nice relaxing home-cooked dinner, Algerian dessert, and a bottle of Rosé.

Lis has a big day at Giverny tomorrow, so it's early to bed, early to rise for her trip of a lifetime to the country garden home of impressionist Claude Monet.

France beat Romania in soccer tonight. And how we know this is because every time France scored or almost scored, loud cheers billowed up to our third floor room from the packed out bar down a side street. Who says the French aren't patriotic? Allez Bleu!!!

We've been doing a lot of planning on our time off for the things we'll need when we get home: things like water, electric, ride from the airport, a home, and movers, it's quite exhausting.

Paris Metro stop in St. Germain with the Conciergerie and Sainte-Chapelle in the distance

The chapel inside Versailles, France

Versailles Gardens

Musée d'Orsay with flood waters
Paris, France

Inside Musée d'Orsay
Paris, France

Chapter 14

Winding Down

Lisa to Giverny While Mike Rests at Île De La Cité

Semedi, 11 Juin 2016 (Saturday, June 11)

I escorted Lis on the Metro to the travel agent office near the Louvre where she'll pick up her fancy double decker bus to Giverny. After dropping Lis off, I walked about three blocks to the Square du Vert-Galant. It's the point of the Île de la Cité, an island in the middle of the Seine that takes the brunt of the current and splits the river in half. Le Square resembles the front of a ship from above and one of the coolest places to hang out and watch the tourist barges go by. The area was grey and dirty this day, because just last week it was under about five feet of murky flood water.

While taking in the moment, I met an old koala bear herder from Australia at the Square. She claims to have also taught French

Down Under and been to Paris more than thirty times. Sheila's every bit of seventy years old, that's nine in kangaroo years, but full of piss and vinegar. She's a feisty one, I'll tell ya. I felt bad for Sheila this day, she's a half hour late for her French date who left twenty-nine minutes ago, and she's fit to be tied, poor thing. It was nice chatting with an English speaker for a change, well Australian, it's almost English, and it felt good. It's a welcome feeling to converse in your own language after struggling with French for a long time.

Visiting Giverny was huge on Lisa's bucket list to see. After studying Claude Monet's impressionist paintings in school, she has always wanted to see his home and garden, especially since she loves gardening. Monet designed and planted most of his garden himself, and then painted scenes of it. When Lis checked in at the Paris City Tours office, she was overcome with how stuffy and hot it was in the waiting area. The French really don't like fresh air or to use air conditioning!

Lis decided to wait for the bus outside in fresh air. While in line, she met a friendly lady named Kathy from Littleton, Colorado. Kathy was also traveling alone, so they sat together and chatted it up for the one and a half hour ride.

It felt good for Lis to get out of the city and into the countryside for the day. Giverny is a small town at the edge of Normandy. Monet discovered it as he rode by on a train and fell in love with the area. As the bus neared Giverny, it started to downpour, ugh, rain again!

Lis was really hoping to get some great photos of Monet's garden. Everyone was given headsets so they could listen to information in their own language as they walked through the garden. The tour guide took them by the waterlily pond with the rebuilt green Japanese bridge. This bridge is seen in several of his most famous paintings.

Afterwards, she happened on the picturesque cottage gardens near the house. Most people toured the house right away, because it was still raining, which made it overcrowded. Lis waited until right before leaving, which turned out great, because she was able to go in with less people and see the rooms in peace.

Lis was able to explore on her own for 1.5 hours before going back onto the bus. She wandered through Monet's garden, clicking pictures as fast as possible, all the while trying to remember the exact spots where Monet painted some of her favorite paintings. She was overjoyed to find a lot of them!

Finally the rain subsided, and the sun broke through the clouds. Lis scurried about the gardens again to capture the same scenes in different lighting.

The peaceful two acre property was teeming with flowers, rows upon rows of gorgeous blooms in varying kinds and colors, some weaving their way up trellises and arbors. The center of the garden had a wider walkway lined with arbors of roses going all the way down to a green gate. The place smelled heavenly!!

Monet's famous waterlily pond is located on the other side of a road and has to be accessed through a tunnel under the busy road. Claude diverted part of the nearby Epte River to create a peaceful lush oasis. At first, he encountered opposition for the project, but once the official in charge found out he was the famous artist, all objections subsided tout de suite.

Lis was surprised, expecting a more abundant number of waterlilies. She was able to walk across Monet's famous green Japanese arched bridge and around the whole pond, just taking in all the magic. She preferred his cottage gardens at the house over the pond due to the color and scents of the abundant flora.

With time running out, Lis whisked through Monet's house, spending only seconds in each room before returning to the bus. Unfortunately the tour was limited to two hours at the property. His expansive country house was pale rose, accented with green shutters, and with five chimneys to keep the family warm in the long northern European winters. The interior rooms reflected the cheerful hues of his garden.

The yellow dining room was warm and inviting, while the kitchen was surrounded in cool blue and white ceramic tile. The oversized gas stove was comprised of more burners than the average modern Parisian apartment today. His two kids and her six made good use of this well-equipped kitchen.

The heart of the house was the master's studio, naturally lit with high ceiling. You could just imagine Monet, brush in hand, working on one of his masterpieces.

Lis exited the house, walked through the garden, turned around, and while facing the house, she is magically transported into "Garden Path at Giverny", one of Monet's famous works.

With no time left to amble through her garden dreamworld, Lis had to catch the bus before it left without her. She could not afford to miss the bus; the train workers were on strike and taxis non-existent.

The tour guide earlier explained to everyone to exit out the rear of the gift shop, bearing left until a side street, and left again where they would be met by her and directed to the bus. Making her last turn, Lis was shocked to discover the tour guide missing. Fearing she missed her ride, Lis approached a local who, seeing the terror in her face, directed her to bus parking where she hustled and made it just in time. Contemplating what just happened, Lis concluded the missing tour guide threw her off course.

Immediately after running in the cold, dank air, Lis's resilient cough came back. She was very frustrated about that; however, she was absolutely thrilled to have seen Monet's gardens and experience the beautiful countryside where he lived. Another one "off the bucket list", she whispered.

On the way back to Paris, Lis sat again with Kathy and listened as she explained how life has changed in her area of town from population growth and Littleton culture since her state legalized marijuana. Another American tourist sitting across from them was originally from Colorado, so they swapped war stories of their hometowns while Lis snacked on her jellybeans. :)

The bus dropped everyone off at the stuffy tourist office, Lis said goodbye to Kathy, and walked to the nearest Metro stop. She took line 7 from the Louvre six stops straight to Rue Monge. Her journey home went smoothly, and twenty minutes after getting off the bus, a quick chin rub to Snowflake, she walked into the apartment.

Resting and Yucky Weather
Dimanche, 12 Juin 2016 (Sunday)

Both of our old bodies are exhausted, but Lis went to Giverny yesterday, and I hibernated in the apartment. The house moving, endless travel, running around, weather, travel anxiety, etc. is finally catching up to us. It feels a lot like the malaise of jet lag, but it's life lag. I took it easy this Dimanche day, but Lis pushed it one more excursion than she should have, and now needs to head back to her doctor. Yes, she has a doctor in Paris, actually she has two.

With the Apres Futbol tournament here in France, Paris has been invaded by hordes of smiling, laughing, extroverted, singsongy Irish futbol fans. Ireland plays Sweden in a match this Monday. They're the talk of the town, almost celebrities on the local TV and newspapers. The normally stoic Parisians are getting a kick out of the opposite end of the personality spectrum.

An interesting thing happened pertaining to our living situation back in Florida. We were getting frustrated trying to get a copy of the lease from Karl, the owner of the temporary beach condo. We gave Karl our old property manager, Vince, as a reference. We had a great working relationship with Vince and had never been late for rent, so he liked us.

Perhaps suspecting this international tenant was a Nigerian scammer, Karl called Vince at his office to make sure we were legitimate. Vince assured him we were real people who presented no trouble. Fearing losing good tenants, Vince jumped on his smartphone and offered us one of his upcoming properties that only became available the day we landed in the States.

Vince offered us a really nice place in a peaceful part of town. It turns out the new rental is bigger than our last house, and in a part of town we were familiar with, so we took it. Sight unseen. Four months ago, we were fully expecting a smaller, more confined rental, so I guess everything worked out for the better.

We informed Karl our former property manager found us a nice place, and we would not be needing his rental. Karl expressed his disappointment in his email, but thanked us for getting back to him. We only found out what transpired behind the scenes when Vince told us his side of the story four days after we got home.

Back in Paris, today's weather is like a recurring bad dream, but we're making the best of it and recharging our batteries for the upcoming big travel day. We'll be needing a lot of energy for the packing, cab, hotel, airport, security, waiting, planes, more planes, customs, driver, moving trucks, strange new house and storage units. I told Lis, "We'll be back in Florida looking at each other and saying, 'Did we really do this? Or did we dream it?'"

I've heard somewhere Paris is like that crazy girlfriend from your past: beautiful, intense, bat shit crazy, while barely escaping with your life. Then to miss her, and you'll do anything to have her back. I definitely understand that quote now.

It's been all worth it: the sickness, bad weather, bathroom shortages, culture shock, crowds, long lines, Metro, pickpockets, language barrier, eternal sea legs, a couple of real smelly people, city life, and lots of dog poop dodging. We're tickled we did it, and can't wait to go back, viva la France!

Resting and Planning Life Back in Florida
Lundi, 13 Juin 2016 (Monday)

Planning for our new place in Florida, we have the water and electric sorted out, lease signed electronically, car insurance reactivated. We just have to get back to familiarity and make it all work.

I swear it's like the movie *Groundhog Day*, pretty crappy today, cold, breezy, and overcast, no wonder the French don't smile much on the street. Ireland tied Sweden 1-1 today; the Irish considered it a great victory, the Swedes a loss.

It always amazes me, many Parisians don't take into account people and their time. I specifically noticed this when it pertains to fellow grocery shoppers and their forward progress.

If you're walking down one of those narrow aisles at your local super marché, a Parisian shopper will open the freezer door and just cut you off from moving down the aisle. If they would have just waited one second, you could have walked right by without interruption.

They seem to be totally oblivious to the human being they just cut off. However, it gets stranger, the now blocked French person will just stand there patiently until the "rude" customer finishes what they are doing. Okay, there's one more level of strangeness. The customer who just cut off the other individual will not be in ANY kind of hurry or show any kind of concern to finish quickly, so that the patiently waiting person can be on their way; no, they will act like nobody's there. My head would flipping explode, or is that just me?

Sometimes when this inconvenience would happen to me, I would say, "Pardon," nudge my way by, and the said offender will appear startled someone would ask them politely to get the hell out of the way; but they temporarily transform into a seemingly concerned person and politely get the hell out of the way. Cultural differences, this one was especially difficult for me.

Lisa Goes Back to the Doctor
Mardi, 14 Juin 2016 (Tuesday)

Before we left to see the doctor, we translated exactly what we needed to tell him. Google translates French into the more formal written language. The spoken language has numerous amounts of slang and contractions that have been chopped off and squished together. It turns multiple words into an amalgamation of slurred, sometimes unintelligible squishiness. This can be almost impossible for the non-native or beginning speaker to understand.

People here, and I guess everywhere, really appreciate it when you attempt their language no matter how bad it is. Many locals understandably get a little miffed if a foreigner expects a local to speak English right off the bat, and I can't say I blame them. Bonjour, with the proper inflection, can bring a smile to some of the most hardened francophones.

Back up Rue Monge to the familiar Doctor's office. Opening the waiting room door, Lis was greeted by seven downcast, sullen faced, sickly souls. "This won't be as fast as last time." Almost everyone in the waiting room had a cough. The cold, damp weather is getting even some of the hardiest locals sick! Thankfully one elderly lady in the waiting room spoke English. She graciously informed Lis when it was her turn.

Again, there is no receptionist, the doctor is a one man show here. When the doctor is pleased, he opens the door, looks around to see who gets up next, and ushers them in. Everyone was aware and respectful of the proper order of who was next, so everything ran smoothly.

Seeing the doctor spends about five to ten minutes with each person, Lis estimated she had at least a thirty-five minute wait ahead of her. Sitting there in another stuffy room with no air conditioning, Lis marveled at the tiny window and was thankful it was open for the little bit of fresh air it surrendered.

When it was finally her turn, Lis showed the doctor her Google translation, stating her reappearing symptoms being the reason she was back. The doctor, upon reading the note to himself, raised one of his eyebrows, reared up in his chair, shoulders back, cleared his throat, and in French recited this finely crafted opus. He enunciated as if the note was the most exquisite of poetry, using hand gestures and acting out each and every verb. Shivering when she inferred it was cold, huffing with moving arms when she ran at Giverny, and coughing when she stated such. It was a regular comedy hour performance. I don't know who enjoyed it more?

The doc asked Lis if she wrote it? "Yes, with the help of Google Translate on the computer." The doc finished his show by explaining all the instructions to her in French. Lis just stared at him with a smile and the face you have when you have no idea what another person is saying, but want to get out of there.

Thankfully Lis and the Doc were able to exchange enough information to make it work. He did, however, speak a few English words at the end. Upon leaving, he asked her where she lived, and when she said, "Florida," his eyes beamed, he took in a big breath and let it out slow, and with a deep yearning he said, "Oh, where it's sunny everyday!"

"Yes, and I miss the sun so much."

Doc said she'll be feeling fine once she gets home, yes, to warm tropical weather, and he was right.

After the medical instructions were over, the doctor took out his smartphone and showed Lis pictures of the Seine River flooding. She was puzzled he took the time to do this, knowing there were several other patients waiting to see him. You may have to wait for service in France, but it's great and focused when you get it. Lis considered it an honor he spent the extra time.

The doctor went on to say how it's been many years since the Seine flooded that bad. Back in 1930 and again in the 80's, there was massive flooding, but the worst was 1910 when the water was twenty feet above normal, and muddy water flowed freely down the nearby streets.

During our time in Paris, we witnessed the Seine rise fifteen feet above normal; however, the water didn't crest the massive retaining wall that holds back the river. The doctor filled out the prescription for antibiotics, nasal decongestant, and an expectorant. We paid him €25, said "Merci," and headed home. On the way home, we stopped in the pharmacy to fill the prescriptions, our total was 16 euros for all three medicines.

Later that evening, after resting, we took one last stroll down the trendy cafe road, Rue Mouffetard, for one last time. We meandered down the cobblestone street, taking in the sights, smells, and sounds of this youthful cafe culture. Losing track of our wanderings, we somehow found ourselves in the middle of a typical French labor demonstration.

With the traffic cordoned off, the road was filled with raucous city workers parading down the avenue waving signs, holding flares, blowing horns, yelling into megaphones, and the occasional heart stopping bomb-like firecracker. Leading the way were multiple little red and white cars with rowdy strikers hanging out the windows. Litter was everywhere. I thought, *maybe they were the street cleaners?*

The local drivers seemed really annoyed they had to detour around the demonstrators, but this is France. It's not like they've never seen a strike before. Getting detoured by the parade and lost, we came across a bus stop with a street map behind glass, so we got our bearings and made our way home.

More Bad Weather So We Rest in Our Apartment
Mercedi, 15 Juin 2016 (Wednesday)

We cleaned the apartment, packed most of our clothes, made our final trash run, finished off any scraps of leftover food, and mentally prepared for what lays ahead of us in way of travel and tasks we'll need to do once we get back to Florida. We're still trying to figure out if the taxis are on strike here in Paris. There were threatening rumors floating around earlier this week.

Square du Vert-Galant
It's the point of the Île de la Cité, an island in the middle of the Seine.
Paris, France

Claude Monet's home and gardens
Giverny, France

Claude Monet's waterlily pond and bridge
Giverny, France

Claude Monet's garden
Giverny, France

Fromage (cheese) shop
Rue Mouffetard, Paris, France

Chapter 15

Au Revoir Paris

Checking Out of Our Paris Apartment and Checking Into
Hotel at Paris Airport
Thursday, June 16

We finished packing and polished off or threw out the last
bits of food lingering around. Down the elevator, and an emotional
farewell with Snowflake, our beautiful apartment mascot and
protector. She winked at us (no really she did) with her beautiful
green eyes. She knew it was time, so did we. We gave her a little
rub under her chin and said au revoir. For the last time, we
descended the steps, out the door, and up to the Rue Monge taxi
stand.

As we approached the taxi stand, we could make out at least
five vehicles waiting for their next fare. Thank God no strike. Rule

of thumb, you must take the first taxi in line that has its rooftop light illuminated, or you'll get reprimanded. "Bonjour," I handed the driver the address for the Charles De Gaulle Ibis airport hotel, he nodded in agreement and set the meter. There are no atheists in foxholes or Parisian taxis, I always say. Only one hundred fifty new grey hairs later, we arrive safely, though a little shaken, at the right hotel.

The Ibis was really nice: bright lights, lots of windows, modern furniture, three restaurants, WiFi, free shuttle to Terminal 1, all for under a Franklin a night. This place was the closest thing to a real "mall" we've encountered in Paris. We could have used a place like the Ibis during all the rain, just to hang out.

This hotel operated two restaurants and a small deli in the lobby, which were very convenient; however, both restaurants closed between 2:30-7:00 pm which was not so convenient. Most French restaurants were closed during these hours, but at an airport hotel where people are arriving from all over the world? If an airline passenger who just arrived from far away is starving for a meal, that famished person will have to wait five hours for a restaurant to open, or head into town only to find those restaurants are closed also. They would just have to settle for a cold pre-made snack at the deli.

Our last lunch in Europe consisted of pizza at the Italian restaurant, since it hadn't closed yet, but it was a long taxing wait for service. Service was so slow, the locals were complaining about the service, it was that bad. We've found the servers in France get to you when they get to you, and not a second before. When they do finally reach you, they make your needs the highest priority, and that part was refreshing.

Now the shuttle to Terminal 1 is in the train station attached to our hotel, so after lunch we surveyed our route to be prepared for tomorrow's flight. Crossing paths with mobs of incoming tourists, we scouted and found the correct underground shuttle. It was a surprise to find an escalator, but lo and behold, the one going to our shuttle was closed for repairs, could you imagine that? Looks like we will have to carry our bulky luggage down steps one more time tomorrow, just for giggles!

Needing to print our paperwork for the flight tomorrow, the lobby printer malfunctioned, so Lis inquired at the receptionist, and was instructed to email our boarding passes to her, and she would print them from her printer. After completing our boarding passes, we hung out in the lobby and watched all the bright-eyed rookies getting off the shuttle. Newbies, they're so cute! Back to the room, recheck our arrangements back in Florida, and relax.

Weary of the long waits, for dinner that evening, we attempted to order a meal from the lobby bar since the other restaurants were, of course, closed. Reading the bar menu, we learned you can order food 24/7. When we inquired of this, the barista had a confused look, like we were asking for a 24 oz. medium rare Kobe beef filet mignon, smothered with saffron-infused Morel mushrooms. His semi-shocked facial expression implied, he wasn't sure if they served any food or what exactly food was. I guess 24/7 kitchen hours were not hours in a row?

With hunger demons clawing at our insides, I asked again, and he mumbled, "Let me check." He opened the freezer right behind him and surprise, lo and behold, wouldn't you know, there were bags of prepared frozen food inside. Pulling out a frozen bag of meat and veggies, he asked, "Is this what you want?"

"How the hell would I know, it's in an unmarked bag?" My stomach interrupted my brain; sure, we were so hungry and just wanted something.

The head chef and bartender confidently microwaved our frozen gourmet masterpiece right in front of us. With astute timing and the greatest of skill, he emptied the scalding hodgepodge of meat and pasta into a disposable styrofoam bowl. Famished, we hurried our culinary masterpiece back to our private cubby hole by the bar and feasted. As it turned out, our meal was what we attempted to order in the first place, and to be honest, wasn't too bad!

Flying from Paris to Tampa, Arrive in USA!
Friday, June 17

Rising early to catch the 7 am shuttle to Charles de Gaulle airport, we passed through security with ease and located our gate. We snacked on a granola bar in our room for morning fuel, and later purchased a real breakfast in the terminal. Charles de Gaulle airport is huge, but well marked. It seemed to take us about a half hour to get from our shuttle to security.

Bathroom Report from the Paris Charles de Gaulle Airport: Lis needed the little girl's room right before boarding our big flight to Newark, but a maintenance man was working right in front of the ladies' room door. Seeing the expression on Lis's face, he pointed at the men's room as if to say, "You can go in there, you're still in France."

"What, what, what, no way, Pierre, I'm not going in the men's room, there's men in there!"

Around the same time of all this bathroom confusion, Lis noticed a family bathroom for moms with little children. Feeling as though she ducked a bullet, she crept in figuring it would be like the ones in the U.S. It had a diaper changing table and full-sized sink, but the only toilet was child size, like teeny-tiny size for potty training. The potty was so small, she stood there in shock, "There's just no way." Foiled again, she ended up waiting for the maintenance man to finish the ladies' room. While leaving the big girl potty, another woman walked into the family bathroom and walked right back out.

Sitting at our terminal, and I'm starting to miss Paris with all its nasty weather and cultural differences.

We flew out of Charles de Gaulle Airport with United on a Boeing 777. I love love love the 777, or at least this configuration of it. I sat in the first seat in business class with three in row, which means no seat ahead of me, so plenty of leg room. Besides, I can keep an eye on first class.

Woo woo, first class is sweet, that's the way to travel. The seats in first class on this 777 were like RV captain chairs that envelope you in cushiony goodness, warmth, and love, well maybe not love.

Bathroom Report: United had a bevy of stewards and stewardesses waiting on first class hand and foot. Although I didn't see any foot massages, I could not see everything, so I'm not sure. I witnessed one of the first class stewards rebuff an attempted bathroom foray by one of the unwashed from economy. First class bathroom security was vigilant and determined, but at the perfect time, in-between shifts, when nobody's looking, and you're fast enough, you never know. Seinfeld was right, first class bathrooms ARE like an English garden. ;-)

The flight went well, we dozed off often for short catnaps. We didn't take advantage of all the movies the plane offered till two hours before landing. For most of the way, we listened to 60's, 70's, and 80's music on headphones while longing for the Florida warmth and sunshine. Hell, we'll take New Jersey warmth and overcast right now.

Our flight continued for seven and a half hours, and this plane made that type of travel drudgery into a minor but extended inconvenience. United and the Boeing 777 were a match made in heaven for this long distance haul. We had a great experience.

Landing in Newark, we needed to go through customs before we caught our flight to Tampa. Disembarking off the plane, we caught a breath of our country's air, and we could feel warm life reenergizing our bodies.

At customs, the primary line was long, and when we ultimately arrived to the front of the primary line, there was a young, dark-skinned Indian man directing each group to one of the appropriate fifteen secondary lines. Upon receiving our paperwork, the young man glanced at our passports, motioned with his open hand to line 6 and said, "Welcome home." I know he says that hundreds of times a day, but it hit me. I have to admit, my heart welled up a bit. It's great to travel, but it's awesome to be home. Sometimes it's great to leave just to get the warm squishy feeling when you get off the plane in your own country.

Our next plane from Newark to Florida was how you say the "stripped down economy model", it was an Airbus 319. I never heard of the 319, a 320, and 330, but this 319 was bare bones, baby. It's like the type of Chevys delivery companies buy without radios, electric windows, and no air conditioner. This 319 is what we were unceremoniously packed into to fly from Newark to Tampa, and that flight wasn't as spacious or comfortable, and no fancy lavender-scented bathrooms.

Speaking about Airbus, while gallivanting around Charles de Gaulle airport, I came upon for the first time in person the Airbus A380, and oh sweet baby Jesus, that thing blew my mind. He was a handsome four engine Thai Air behemoth, posing on the tarmac like a prize bull. Unfortunately we didn't observe it fly, so I'm not sure it could?

We finally arrive in Tampa, and the wonderful driver we found on Craigslist waited at baggage claim to claim us. Our driver, Rob, spoke perfect English with a slight Michiganese accent.

Driving home from Tampa airport was a misty-eyed homecoming for us. Though we weren't gone long (nine weeks), gazing out the window at our home landscape and culture, the feeling was a sentimental heart-tugger.

Rob, our angel, gladly took us to our indoor storage unit, so we could retrieve the key to the outdoor unit one mile away. He then drove us to the outdoor unit so we can pick up our car. We were touched when Rob apologized for not having jumper cables, which we thankfully didn't need. You were great, big guy!

We strategically pre-packed the car with the articles we'd need for our first night back. We drove down the old familiar roads to our new, never seen, empty rental. Pulling into a strange driveway, double-checking the address, Lis got the house key from the lock box, and for the first time, we went inside.

Walking into our strange new house, head in a fog, we were met with an unusual gust of hot air, so I turned on the air conditioner, and it didn't work. We plugged in the coffee maker, unpacked the toiletries, explored a little, inflated our temporary blow up bed, and passed out for the night. Lis said I was snoring before my head hit the pillow.

Not knowing up from down, left from right, we're going to need a good night's sleep so we can get up the next day, drive to the storage units, and pack the car with the first of many loads. Each trip will slowly bring our lives back to a semblance of normal with the creature comforts we formally took for granted.

The place was nice and spacious, our furniture will have a little breathing room here. It's our all time favorite layout with enough closet space for all of Lisa's photos. I may even get a closet for myself in one of the spare bedrooms.

With my body still on European time, I'd wake up the next day long before sunrise and head to the storage unit just as it opened at 6 am. I filled the car with kitchen stuff, toiletries, clothes, now luxuries to us. Getting home before Lis awoke, I began the long task of turning this house into a home.

Seeing building activity around where we relocated our banana plants, we hustled over on the first Sunday and rescued our thriving, healthy plants. Yeah, they survived and no arrests!

We are complete zombies, and if you know what jet lag is, you'll understand, it's "awesome-lee-crappy". For weeks following the trip, I will be getting up between 1 and 3 am and meandering around the house looking for something to do.

Back Home in Florida
June 18,19,20

The air conditioning was still broke, it was 91 in the house when we arrived; but after being in the damp, cold, frozen wasteland of northern Europe, the "heat" was kind of "appreciated". We notified Vince, our property manager, and his air conditioning mechanic rushed out to jump start the air conditioning tout de suite.

Everything in Florida is open most of the time, most restaurants don't close for five hours after lunch, people smile and make casual eye contact for no reason, we are driving an automobile in the familiar countryside, we hear English everywhere, houses are bigger than a refrigerator box, elevators are bigger than a coffin, escalators go up and down, grocery stores are "gihunormous", and Lisa's not coughing. . . . God, it's good to be home.

Home in the Warm Florida Weather
July 14

Yesterday we checked the weather in Paris, and the high this JULY day was 61 degrees, cloudy, and rain. The same day it's going to be 67 and sunny in Iceland. Iceland, for the love of God, "Ice" is in the name of the country, and it's warmer than Paris!! I investigated when I got home, and realized Paris is on the same latitude as the border of the U.S. and Canada. Paris is more north than Fargo, North Dakota, and St. Paul, Minnesota, nuff said!

This trip to France was awesome, though it may sound like I grumbled a lot. The cold, damp weather really beat both of us up so bad, it shortened our travel plans. I'm a sunshine dependent person, and might get a little grumpy when I don't have enough. Please forgive me if I took any magic away from France, it's a great country with incredible people which I respect more now than before. Yes, we ran into a few clunkers, but I run into plenty of them here in the U.S.

I hope I can make it back to Europe in the future. If it can be arranged, I'd love to visit Paris again and go back to that Algerian bakery for another three slices of baklava for Lis and I. Wink, Wink!

About the Author

Michael A. Barry

Michael A. Barry is a semi-retired small business owner,
husband, and world traveler from Philadelphia,
Pennsylvania now living in Florida.
Hobbies include: aviation, anthropology, psychology,
history, and weekend polyglot.

barry_michael99@yahoo.com

I hope you can still feel the awe of the magnificent architecture,
taste the pastries and baguettes, and feel the sway of the Metro train
as it passes under the Louvre.
For more pictures and helpful hints on traveling France go to
www.facebook.com/VagabondsinFrance

To rate this book on Amazon go to:
http://www.amazon.com/dp/B01NCUNSEK
To rate it on Goodreads go to: www.goodreads.com

Made in the USA
Lexington, KY
12 September 2017